UMASS RISING

THE UNIVERSITY OF MASSACHUSETTS AMHERST AT 150

KATHARINE GREIDER

AUTHOR'S NOTE

The author is grateful to the many UMass Amherst students, alumni, former and present faculty, and staff members who generously gave their time to help tell the story of the university over the past 150 years. Their efforts have enriched this book in incalculable ways.

In the making of this book, dozens of people shared their memories and insights. While only a fraction of their personal stories are in these pages, the feelings and thoughts of all we interviewed informed every aspect of the creation of *UMass Rising*. We hope that this publication honors the experiences of all those connected with UMass Amherst as we celebrate this remarkable institution's sesquicentennial.

— Katharine Greider

ISBN 978-1-55849-989-8

Published by the University of Massachusetts Amherst in celebration of the sesquicentennial of its founding.
Distributed by
University of Massachusetts Press
East Experiment Station
671 North Pleasant Street
Amherst, MA 01003
www.umass.edu/umpress

Text written by Katharine Greider
Project-managed, edited, designed, and produced by Vern Associates, Inc., Amesbury, Massachusetts
Printed and bound by C&C Offset Printing Company, Hong Kong

CONTENTS

INTRODUCTION

From its humble beginnings as Massachusetts Agricultural College to its present standing as a world-class research institution, the University of Massachusetts Amherst has always had, at its heart, a powerful guiding principle: that all people, regardless of wealth or social status, should have the opportunity to pursue an excellent college education. For 150 years, through periods of social upheaval and economic hardship, in wartime and peace, through eras of explosive growth and sharp decline, the University of Massachusetts Amherst has remained a driving force in the democratization of higher education, all while serving the Commonwealth through its life-changing research.

UMass Rising is a sweeping history of the role that our great university has played on a grand stage, but it is also more than that. It presents stories that we may not have heard before and others that are told in new ways. It tells the story of how our founders negotiated the landscape to create the campus and why its original footprint was shaped like an elm leaf; of how our early students labored as "farmboys" and rode trolleys from one end of campus to the other. It tells of dance cards and bonfires, the proscriptions of behavior for the first women on campus and the "Rage in the Cage." It also tells how familiar, treasured aspects of UMass Amherst—the campus pond, the ancient beech trees at the Durfee Conservatory, the stunning architecture of our buildings—came to be.

In the following pages, you will read about the impressive work of our faculty and students. You will see that our innovative spirit is far reaching and has brought the university to new heights of global relevance. You will learn that our devotion to advancing the human condition through teaching, research, and service remain undiminished over the decades.

Founded as a result of the Morrill Act of 1862, UMass Amherst was built on the premise that the discoveries we make—and the knowledge we create—should improve the quality of life for citizens of the Commonwealth and beyond. The range of our impact and influence as the Commonwealth's land-grant university is beyond anything our founders could have imagined.

UMass Rising documents the journey of an institution that, in its 150-year pursuit of discoveries to make the world a better place, has never deviated from its commitment to excellence and access. It is my honor as Chancellor of this great university to share with you this remarkable story.

Kumble R. Subbaswamy
Chancellor, University of Massachusetts Amherst

UMASS RISING

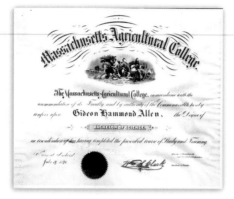

1862 Abraham Lincoln signs the Morrill Land-Grant Act

1863 Governor Andrew signs charter for the Massachusetts Agricultural College (M.A.C.)

1864 Amherst townspeople vote to raise subscription for the new college

- Henry Flagg French becomes first president of M.A.C.

1866 Paul A. Chadbourne is named second president

1867 William Smith Clark succeeds Chadbourne

- M.A.C.'s faculty of four greets first students

- Tuition = $36 per annum

1869 *The Index* begins publication

1870 Tuition rises to $54

1871 First commencement: 27 B.S. degrees

- M.A.C. crew defeats Harvard and Brown

1872 M.A.C. enrollment = 171

1873 Tuition rises to $75

1875 First woman admitted (as "select," or nondegree, student)

1876 Clark establishes agricultural college in Hokkaido, Japan

1879 Charles L. Flint succeeds Clark

- Tuition falls to $36

1880 Levi Stockbridge becomes president

1882 Massachusetts Agricultural Experiment Station established

- Liberal arts offerings added to curriculum

1883 James Greenough assumes presidency

1886 Stone chapel dedicated

- Henry Hill Goodell becomes president

UMASS

THE UNIVERSITY OF MASS

1888 Hatch Experiment Station established

1890 *Aggie Life* begins publication

- Two-year practical agriculture course established

1892 Campus pond created

1895 Massachusetts Agricultural and Hatch Experiment Stations merge

1896 First master's degrees awarded

1899 Free tuition for U.S. citizens established

1901 Two female students enroll, becoming first women to receive degrees from M.A.C. (class of '05)

- First professional coaches hired

- *Aggie Life* retitled *College Signal*

1902 Warren Hinds receives first doctorate awarded by M.A.C.

- Varsity basketball introduced

1903 Goodell introduces first majors: agriculture, horticulture, biology, chemistry, math, and landscape gardening

1904 Mathew Washington Bullock first black coach salaried by integrated American college

1906 Kenyon Butterfield replaces Goodell as president

1908 Graduate School established as a separate entity

1909 College extension service established

1910 Ten fraternities in place

1911 Academic restructuring divides 23 departments into 5 basic divisions

1912 Free tuition restricted to Massachusetts residents

- Five women enrolled at M.A.C.

RISING

HUSETTS AMHERST AT 150

"Educated labor and intelligent industry may walk with kings and princes as their peer."

—*Special report of the trustees of Massachusetts Agricultural College, 1864*

HIGHER LEARNING FOR THE COMMONWEALTH

A Public College in Amherst

HE HORSES CHURNED UP DUST AS THEY TURNED WEST OFF THE MAIN ROAD FROM AMHERST AND PULLED UP BESIDE THE FIRST HUMBLE BUILDINGS OF THE MASSACHUSETTS AGRICULTURAL COLLEGE.

One by one the young men descended from stagecoaches and gigs, some in good woolen suits, others in coarse homespun. There were thirty-four in all. All but two were sons of the Commonwealth. A few hailed from the eastern part of the state, but more than a dozen had grown up within 25 miles of Amherst. Most had some experience working on a farm.

So they would have had some idea how to assess the property they surveyed that October morning of 1867. It was an agglomeration of five farms that had lain idle for some years. The main road through campus, North Pleasant, traveled along a central bench of relatively flat terrain. To the east were hills covered here and there with a patch of woods or scraggly apple orchard. To the west the terrain sloped off into scrub and swamp. The parcel of some 300 acres was crisscrossed with tumbledown split-rail fences.

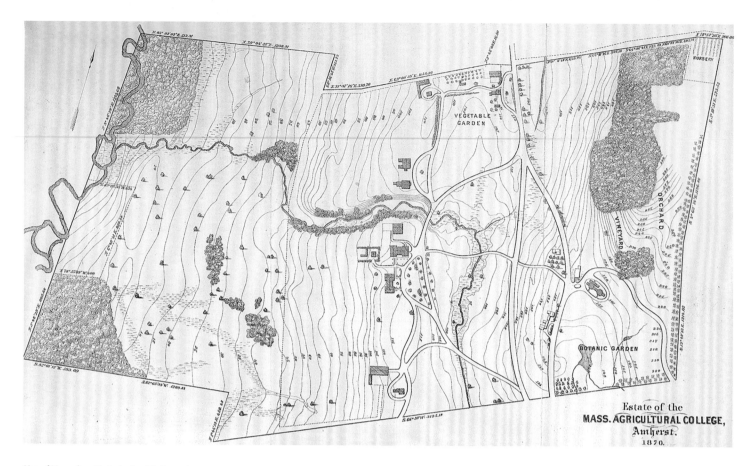

Map of Massachusetts Agricultural College, 1870s

William S. Clark

(Previous page) The campus as it appeared to the first students at Massachusetts Agricultural College: a wide space of farm and field with a few buildings scattered about. At this early date, two roads already divided M.A.C. into what was called the east and west campuses, forming a shape that looks appropriately like the leaf of an elm tree.

As for buildings, they were a work in progress; in the estimation of one reporter from New York City, the place looked like a brickyard. South College, a red brick dormitory and classroom building with gabled roof and corner tower, stood to the west of the road, ready for business. Not far to the north was a two-story chemistry lab that would do double duty as a chapel, and a little farther still, across a ravine that drained a brook that ran through the property, was an old farmhouse where students would be fed. Within a year or so would come another "boarding club" next to the first, and a second dorm and classroom building, North College. For now, though, the elegant glass conservatory at the foot of the hills to the east was nearing completion, a testament to the vaulting ambitions of the college founders. Soon to be filled with exotic banana trees, cacti, and orchids, the Durfee Plant House was inspired by one in London's famous Kew Gardens.

Faculty awaiting their young charges numbered four. There was the strapping, blue-eyed William S. Clark, president and professor of botany and horticulture, whom a student would later remember as "ardent, impetuous, sanguine, often rash, overflowing with fun, wit, and humor," his lectures in chemistry "punctuated by loud explosions." Henry H. Goodell, professor of rhetoric and modern languages, would be known for his fair-minded discipline and dedication to the college library. A shy, kind little man by the name of Ebenezer Strong Snell would teach math. And Levi Stockbridge, a local farmer and self-made intellectual with sharp features and wiry build, would superintend the school's "model farm," teaching agriculture as a science, an art, and a high calling.

The examination for admission took place in the afternoon. It was lengthy, but in the end no one was refused a spot. The faculty had advertised the college as a good place for

Professor Levi Stockbridge (inset) and planting corn with the class of 1882 (top)

youth who couldn't afford the state's elite private colleges. These educators were likely every bit as eager as their students—all had thrown in their lots together. Classes would begin the next day, October 2.

NEW THINGS UNDER THE SUN

They were embarking on a bold experiment. Publicly sponsored education for all was a novel idea generated in the heat and optimism of the American experiment itself. For centuries, education beyond childhood had been reserved for a few professionals and the wealthy—people who, as one Harvard professor had famously quipped, could confine their exertions to digging Sanskrit roots.

But this didn't sit well with a people steeped in the egalitarian principles of their young republic, who believed the success of the nation itself depended on the uplift and self-determination of ordinary citizens. "Educated labor and intelligent industry," as the new agricultural college's own trustees had written, "may walk with kings and princes as their peer[s]." Stockbridge would exhort his first incoming class to consider that the only schooling worthy of their proud Commonwealth was "*universal education . . .* dispensing its privileges equally to high & low, the rich and poor, the foreign and native born." The first public high school in Amherst had opened in 1861. And now a college for farmboys! It was a start.

Massachusetts Agricultural College (M.A.C.) also was founded in a belief that modern science—then in the midst of a showy blossoming—could improve the lot of human beings. In fact the founders thought scientific research and study could go a long way toward addressing a serious problem unfolding right there in the hills of western Massachusetts. The land depleted from repeated cropping (not to mention hilly and littered with stones), farm families were abandoning their homesteads in droves for the flat, rich loam of the plains or heading to the mills and factories of industrializing towns and cities. M.A.C.'s founders thought that scientific, progressive farming would help local farmers prosper long after the western frontier had closed.

A few years after opening day, amid the torchlight and jubilation of M.A.C.'s very first commencement, devoted trustee Marshall P. Wilder would exult over the class of 1871. "We shall have among our yeomanry such farmers as the world never before witnessed," he told the assembled graduates, "men who will honor their vocation and therefore be honored by society—the chiefs of our land, the bulwark of our nation."

These high, fine ideas were in the air. But from the beginning, M.A.C.'s students were well aware that not everyone subscribed to them. The *New England Farmer* had predicted the college would be little more than an "apple of discord" among politicians and intellectuals, an "object of merriment" to actual farmers. Many balked at the cost of subsidizing higher education. Others decried the enterprise as such. As one farmer put it to the *Amherst Record*, "The thing for farmers is muscle and manure—not education."

So perhaps it was with more than the ordinary freshman jitters that the first M.A.C. class pulled up to South College that day in 1867, the surrounding hills and valley touched with the first bright colors of autumn. One wrote that the dorm looked like a prison to

First there was the walk out of doors, the stooping and reaching to pluck a sprig of leaves or scrape the lichen from a tree trunk. Later the collector carefully studied, identified, classified, and finally mounted the specimen for safekeeping in a collection known as an herbarium.

For people of the nineteenth century—and especially among the enthusiastic naturalists of New England—this process was an important way of exploring and knowing the world around them. Herbaria helped describe the flora of a particular locale and establish the habits and ranges of plant species. By the mid-nineteenth century the great museums of

Botanic Museum, herbarium and recitation room

Paris, Berlin, Vienna, and London all had large collections. Henry David Thoreau gathered hundreds of specimens in and around Concord for his herbarium. Amherst's own Emily Dickinson started hers at the age of fourteen, inquiring in a letter to her friend Abiah Root, "Have you made an herbarium yet? I hope you will if you have not, it would be such a treasure to you; most all the girls are making one. If you do, perhaps I can make some additions to it from flowers growing around here."

As soon as Massachusetts Agricultural College opened in 1867, President William S. Clark, an Amherst-trained botanist himself, began amassing the collection that would become the Massachusetts State Herbarium. M.A.C. students were expected to follow his example. For many years, the requirement to present a collection of one hundred to two hundred (the number varied) mounted and classified specimens was a M.A.C. rite of passage. The woods, meadows, and marshes around campus offered ample hunting grounds.

him. "When I landed in front of it," he added, "I thought surely I had got to what people call the jumping off place."

A TUMULTUOUS FOUNDING

The journey to that place—to M.A.C.'s opening day—had itself been long and arduous.

Proposals for an agricultural college had kicked around Massachusetts for decades when, in 1862, federal legislation dropped into the state's lap a gift it could not refuse: 360,000 acres of federal land it could sell to raise funds for the founding of a college "accessible to all, but especially to the sons of toil" in agriculture and manufacturing. The bill's sponsor, Congressman Justin Morrill, was the son of a Vermont blacksmith who regretted having to quit school at fifteen and go to work. On his third attempt, the law

"Mountain days are red letter ones in the routine work," observed an 1898 college catalogue. "Barge loads of young students may often be seen returning from the wilds of Holyoke or of Toby with botany cans filled with specimens."

Susie D. Livers, class of 1907, spent quite a few days in May and June 1904 scouring the hills around campus for unusual plants, perhaps donning a neat shirtwaist and plain skirt for the ramble, her wavy brown hair tucked under a straw hat. More than a century later, 35 of her specimens survive in the university archives.

The class of 1907 in front of the veterinary lab, with one woman—Susie Livers, whose specimens collected in the spring of 1904 survive in the university archives to this day.

In Amherst she found red clover, black huckleberry, and groundnut. In Sunderland, a common club moss trailed along the ground, and a chestnut oak dropped its glossy leaves from on high. In a place called Plumtree Swamp, Livers gathered ground pine and the seven-petaled starflower, and in the ravine just north of the old chem lab grew dwarf blueberry, swamp pink, and flowering wintergreen. Honeysuckle and wild sarsaparilla would represent the rugged "Notch" in the Mt. Holyoke Range south of campus; wild viburnum, Mt. Lincoln to the east; and squaw huckleberry, Sugarloaf in the north.

Not all students relished the project, of course. Given the time required to gather and press specimens, procrastination was deadly. Alert to the commercial possibilities this presented, a couple of students in the class of 1911 offered the requisite number of pressed (but not classified) specimens to classmates for $5. Even then, students got into trouble, being forced at the last minute to press the specimens with a hot flatiron, which affected their color.

One hundred fifty years after Massachusetts established its state college at Amherst, the university's own herbarium is a regional resource containing more than 240,000 specimens—including the collection founded by President Clark in 1867, a physical reminder of what has passed away, and what abides, in the Pioneer Valley.

passed, helped along by the secession of Southern states that had opposed its tendency to empower both the federal government and labor. Abraham Lincoln signed the Morrill Act on July 2, 1862, in the very midst of the Civil War. M.A.C. founders Clark and Goodell both were wearing the Union blue.

Under the law, a tenth of each state's grant could be spent on land, with the rest to act as an income-producing endowment. Massachusetts governor John Andrew argued the money should go to bolster the Bussey Institute, an incipient program at Harvard; a handful of other private colleges also put in bids. But members of the state Board of Agriculture proved influential, and the legislature voted in 1863 to found a new college of agriculture, while giving a third of the endowment to the Massachusetts Institute of Technology for providing the kind of applied technical education that would produce engineers.

M.A.C.'s freshly minted trustees then turned to the politically charged issue of where to site the new college. Lexington, Springfield, Northampton, and Amherst all tossed their hats into the ring. Each municipality agreed (at least in principle) to raise $75,000 for the erection of buildings, a condition of the federal grant. In the spring of 1864 the trustees visited the properties on offer, and voted 10 to 4 for Amherst, "situated," as they noted in a report to the governor, "in an agricultural region of native New England farmers . . . where our students will find sympathy, and see that honest men can thrive by honest labor on the land."

The trustees purchased 310 acres from five owners for nearly $40,000; for the benefit of the new college, trustee Nathan Durfee of Fall River bought an adjoining 73 acres with $8,000 of his own money. After eight contentious public meetings, the townspeople of Amherst in May 1865 voted to tax themselves in the amount of $50,000 for construction; the additional $25,000 (and then some) was supplied by the private donations of Durfee, William Kellogg and Henry F. Hills of Amherst, and Samuel Williston of Easthampton.

A typical early room in South College had a coal stove, oil lamp, and small personal library.

The "iron girdle" apparatus from Clark's paper to the Massachusetts Board of Agriculture and the New England Agricultural Institute (top) and the squash itself, betraying the marks of its one-time restraints (bottom)

In the summer 1875, the Massachusetts Agricultural College assailed by critics on all sides, college president William S. Clark endeavored to grow a very large chili squash.

Technically, it was an experiment, but an experiment that borrowed much from the agricultural fair's merry companionability and the dime museum's bizarre spectacle. This vegetable drew large crowds.

Clark propagated the squash inside a sort of iron girdle rigged to an apparatus that would measure the force of its growth by how much it could lift. By August 31 the expanding squash lifted five hundred pounds. It was frightening, really. In fact, Clark's five-year-old daughter famously told him that if the squash ever escaped its iron cage, it would "go at you." "The lifting power was the greatest after midnight, when the growth of the vine and the exhalation from the foliage was least," Clark wrote in a paper presented to the Massachusetts Board of Agriculture and the New England Agricultural Institute in Worcester.

Finally, on October 31, weighing 47¼ pounds and bursting its stays, the thing "carried" (without "clearly raising") five thousand pounds. Why split hairs? The point was awe. "Life," wrote Clark, "is a molecular force, and exerted its almost irresistible power over an immense surface of cell membrane."

Already its friends had sacrificed a great deal of time and money for the college. But there was one more hurdle to clear before opening day: A dispute developed over the fateful question of where, on the property, to locate the college buildings.

The college's first president, Henry Flagg French, passionately espoused nestling them against the hillside in the northeast of the property, capturing the commanding view of the agricultural valley below. Others, apparently including trustee (later president) William S. Clark, favored the lower central area, a place known as Chestnut Ridge for a majestic specimen that grew near the future site of the campus's famous stone chapel.

Reports by no less than the celebrated designers of New York's Central Park—first Calvert Vaux and colleague Joseph R. Richards, then Frederick Law Olmsted—were brought to bear in favor of the hillside. Edward Dickinson, father of the young poet Emily and an august member of the Amherst community, agreed. Still the Chestnut Ridge partisans produced a longer petition. It was a drawn-out affair, but such was the nature of decision-making in a free society. French resigned in disgust. And up, at last, went South College—that "stately pile"—with no time to spare before the arrival of students.

AN EXCELLENT START

During the 1860s and 1870s, students and faculty together made a start of Massachusetts Agricultural College, establishing its basic routines and traditions, and improving its pastoral New England campus.

The boys rose at half past six, breakfasted at seven, gathered in the chapel for brief devotions, then headed to class. All followed a standard four-year course of study that emphasized techniques in agriculture and horticulture and provided a foundation in the sciences (including chemistry, botany, physiology, and social sciences) and math. The ancient Greek and Latin classics that dominated the traditional liberal arts curricula of other colleges were eschewed in favor of English grammar, German, and French. Within several years of opening day, a handful of new professors joined the faculty, most notably Charles A. Goessmann—"Old Dutchy," as he would be known—in chemistry, who like Clark had been trained in Germany at the University of Göttingen. Tests were oral and performed in front of the class.

"Dear Sister," one young man wrote home in February 1873. "We have finished Geometry and are now beginning to get along in Trigonometry but the whole class are together now and we shall have to go quite slowly. . . . It is very cold here to day. How is it at home? It is time for me to do my chores so I must close."

Afternoon was the time for physical activity—manual labor on the farm or the military drills required under the Morrill law. The drills, led by a U.S. Army officer detailed to the college, consisted of setting-up exercises, movements in formation, mock skirmishes, and the like.

Students had to labor several hours per week on the college farm. Some worked a great deal more to defray their costs at college. M.A.C.'s early classes reclaimed the sprawling acreage from its neglected state with their own hands, arms, and backs. "Does pulverizing the soil fertilize it?" went one of Stockbridge's freshman oral exam questions. The answer was a ringing affirmative, and pulverize the soil they did, not only tilling and preparing vast swaths of ground but pulling down dilapidated fences and outbuildings, digging up the roots of many dozens of old apple trees and hedgerows, and ditching and draining acre after acre of swamp. In an 1872 report to Congress, the federal education commissioner adjudged their labor to be "of the least interesting and most disagreeable kind"—indeed it provoked one of M.A.C.'s first student "strikes" or walkouts—but Stockbridge, a firm believer in the salutary effects of this sort of work, vigorously took part himself.

The supper bell rang at 5:30.

Despite their demanding schedules, M.A.C. men began to enjoy the beginnings of an exuberant, youth-oriented college culture. Within just a few years they had a yearbook, the *Index;* the first two of four very early "secret societies" or fraternities, complete with their mysterious symbols and doings; a choir and glee club; a literary society; a baseball team; and a crew team whose 1871 defeat of Harvard's "Brahmin caste," as a M.A.C. fraternity bulletin put it, was hailed as "a very significant occurrence" by the same top education official who frowned on M.A.C.'s labor requirement.

An early football team, season of 1886, wearing M.A.C.'s first formal uniform

Meanwhile, M.A.C. leaders were stumping all over the countryside for the college, talking it up to agricultural societies, legislators, and prominent families. "Let our rich men come forward and complete the work so well begun," trustee Wilder exhorted. "Let them provide funds for experiments, for books, and for the arboretum and botanic garden."

A FIGHT FOR ITS LIFE

Their ardent pleas for support fell on deaf ears.

The college was running on fumes. Proceeds from the federal land grant were not nearly enough to cover annual operations. And while the Morrill law clearly intended states to establish their colleges on a permanent footing, the Commonwealth had never, in fact, committed itself to maintaining the college. Appropriations were piecemeal. In 1873 a deep, grinding economic depression began, making retrenchment the order of the day among state legislators and farm families alike. To many, college for working people began to seem like an extravagance.

Enrollment, standing at 171 in 1872, plunged, with fewer than 20 freshmen entering in 1875. President Clark waived tuition for the incoming class of 1877, which buoyed attendance, but only temporarily. For some time M.A.C. had hobbled along with the help of trustee William Knowlton, who extended thousands in loans when others would not and paid small bills out of pocket. Stockbridge gave $1,000 to continue faculty experiments. By the end of the decade, the college was in debt to the tune of more than $30,000.

The situation desperate, many called for the state to administer the coup de grâce. An investigation by a handful of alumni yielded a report charging mismanagement. The papers pounced. The *Boston Globe* suggested a bill abolishing the college, the *Post* repeatedly excoriating M.A.C. as an "ill conditioned and profitless enterprise," a "waterlogged and beggarly institution," and a "hungry buzzard." From the governor's office came a proposal to simply fold the ailing M.A.C. into nearby Amherst College. In the midst of all this, President Clark, while indignantly defending the college and its budget in every particular, asked the trustees for a second leave of absence; he'd already spent nearly a year developing an agricultural college in Japan. They refused him, and he resigned.

In April 1879, the legislature enacted a chilling piece of business: It agreed to pay off the college's $32,000 debt but made the volunteer trustees *personally* liable for any future expenditures in excess of income—and charged the governor's council with devising a plan to "finally separate" the college from the state treasury.

The mood on campus was grim indeed. Loyal trustee Charles L. Flint reluctantly agreed to serve as president—without pay. The board slashed salaries and sold 25 animals

Early in the twentieth century, increased enrollment and a broadening educational mission at M.A.C. whipped up school spirit to an almost feverish pitch. "Mass singing" was a popular college pastime, and many young people could read music and compose rhyming verse with the same fluency that twenty-first-century students might exhibit in videos, raps, or Twitter and blog posts. M.A.C. students set to writing new school songs to belt out around a post-game bonfire or festive Commencement Eve table.

Some were gentle paeans like "Dear Old Massachusetts" (F. D. Griggs ['13]) and "Mass. Aggie—Here's to Thee" (which, according to composer W. W. Thayer of the class of 1917, should be delivered *con anima*—with feeling). Others were fight songs deserving of the name. "Charge through the line, now batter down the ends. Fight, fight for every yard," urges the class of 1908's D. P. Miller in his classic of the genre, "On the Field." In its infancy at the time, American football was a rough game that thrilled student fans but was not always smiled upon by administrators.

Chants and special cheers or "yells" were also much in use and popular outlets for student expression.

One yell, sometimes called "The Locomotive," evoked train sounds—the formidable chugging and hissing, punctuated by an occasional shrieking exhalation—that would have been entirely familiar to students who rode in and out of Amherst on the Boston & Maine.

> Mass! Mass! Mass'chusetts!
> Rah! Rah! Rah! Rah!
>
> Mass'chusetts!
> Team! Team! Team!

18

DEAR OLD MASSACHUSETTS

Words and Music by
F. D. GRIGGS
'13

VOICE

There is a cer - tain val - ley, By a riv-er's gold - en

PIANO

strand: Where stands a no - ble col - lege, The

fair - est in the land; Well known through-out our

coun - try, For her truth and loy - al - ty; Old

Copyright MCMXII by Edgar L. Ashley

from the college herd, a move the fraternity publication the *Cycle* condemned as "incomprehensible" given the animals' value, adding that, with all due respect, the editors did not consider Flint up to the job of president. That fall, a mere handful of new students appeared.

M.A.C. held on.

And in 1880, better days came along. Friends of the college rallied. The Alumni Association issued a report advocating its continued independence. People showed up at meetings in Boston and Amherst to protest proposals, such as M.A.C.'s closure or merger with Amherst College. Stockbridge agreed to take over as president. The economy improved, and in 1881, a new governor, John Long, suggested the college might be "fairly entitled . . . to the consideration of the Commonwealth."

UP FROM THE ASHES

Everyone took it as an exceptionally promising omen when, in early 1882, Paul A. Chadbourne agreed to take the helm at M.A.C. In his letter to Chadbourne acknowledging the occasion, acting president Stockbridge was giddy with relief. "Glory!" he wrote. "Hurrah! Hurrah for M.A.C! . . . I don't know what I've written and don't care. I feel good over this day's work and don't you forget it."

Chadbourne already had served a brief term as president before M.A.C.'s opening, then led the University of Wisconsin and later Williams College during a period of rapid growth. He was widely respected in scholarly circles as a deep-thinking naturalist. And he was politically connected, having counted among his friends the recently assassinated President James A. Garfield. Chadbourne planned to broaden M.A.C.'s curriculum to include the liberal arts offerings he believed would allow students to graduate "not only as men of power and practical ability, but as men of learning and culture."

Unfortunately, shortly after bestowing on "Mass Aggie" the prestige of his name, Chadbourne died from a lung ailment that had plagued him since youth. The next president, James Greenough (formerly principal of the Rhode Island Normal School) briefly instituted his curriculum changes. But a more enduring development under Greenough would be the establishment of an experiment station at M.A.C.

The experiment station built on something that had gone *right* at the agricultural college in its most trying years. Its professors had been intent on producing data that would be of practical value to farmers engaged in the hard struggle to make their land pay. Stockbridge, with the help of the class of 1871's William H. Bowker, had invented a series of best-selling specialized fertilizers that protected the soil and boosted crop yields. Goessmann had generated evidence on the viability of the sugar beet as a commercial crop in Massachusetts. Clark had published on the flow of sap in maple trees—information useful to farmers who tapped their trees for that sweet (and lucrative) New England specialty, maple syrup.

In 1882, the Commonwealth recognized these achievements by establishing the Massachusetts Experimental Station on campus (though ostensibly separate from the college). Federal legislation providing research staff at land-grant colleges led to the opening of a second station at M.A.C. in 1888. In 1894, the two merged to form the root of an institution that would thrive for generations.

Meanwhile, campus construction during the 1880s, though not extensive, was significant. The college got labs for entomology and veterinary science. In 1886 the West Experiment Station (used mostly for chemical analysis) became the first building in an area to the northeast of South College, joined in 1889 by the East Experiment Station (devoted mainly to plant pathology and insect control). In his one and only annual report, Chadbourne had asked for a bona fide drill hall and a building ample enough to house a proper library and the public gatherings so crucial to college life. The two-story chemistry building had served all

Boys, be ambitious. Be ambitious not for money or for selfish aggrandizement, not for that evanescent thing which men call fame. Be ambitious for that attainment of all that a man ought to be.
— *William S. Clark*

In the mid-1990s, a newly minted PhD in astronomy from California visited Hokkaido University in Sapporo, Japan, to give a colloquium. In a blog he posted more than a decade later he mentions that the "odd" motto—"Boys, Be Ambitious!"—is practically ubiquitous throughout the campus. He found it particularly telling that one astronomy graduate student actually had the phrase written on a Post-it he had attached to his computer screen.

From the perspective of a late-twentieth-century academic, this may seem surprising, but the phrase became the motto of several institutions in Japan, not least of which is Hokkaido University. It is, in fact, so deeply seated in the Japanese consciousness that a former Japanese prime minister noted that it remains "the best-known English quotation in Japan"—well over a century after its first utterance by none other than William S. Clark, president of the Massachusetts Agricultural College.

The year was 1876. Clark, during a leave from M.A.C., had been hired by the Japanese government to consult on launching Sapporo Agricultural College. Just before embarking on the journey home, he delivered his now-famous farewell exhortation to the Japanese students he'd come to regard with affection and respect.

Clark taught at Sapporo Agricultural College (later Hokkaido University) for only eight months, but he left a deep impression. An intense, voluble man, he'd become something of a controversial figure in Massachusetts, where taxpayers remained unconvinced that they wanted to support his high aspirations for M.A.C. Japan, meanwhile, had a new imperial government intent on modernizing the country to strengthen it against colonialist incursions. The island of Hokkaido, though rich in natural resources, was sparsely populated, underdeveloped, and in need of Clark's know-how. There, among the "Yankees of the East," as Clark would call them, his charisma charmed and inspired.

M.A.C.'s president arrived at Sapporo eager to impart, along with a course of study and modern farming techniques, the republican ideas he saw as the basis for social

these functions, though not well. In 1883, the college had its new drill hall. The following year workmen laid the granite cornerstone of the Romanesque Revival edifice whose impressive steeple would rise high over the M.A.C. campus—and be instantly recognized well over a century later as the very symbol of a proud Commonwealth's thriving public university.

The new stone chapel and library gave the campus a center, a heart. So it was no coincidence that two students in the winter of 1890–91 chose a site beside the chapel to dam up the stream that ran the length of campus. Soon the administration acquired money

progress. Japan's "wonderful emancipation from the tyranny of caste and custom," he enthused at Sapporo's opening ceremonies, "should awaken a lofty ambition in the breast of every student to whom an education is offered."

Clark is said to have displayed his own unconcern for caste and custom by inviting the boys to join him for evening chats during which he sat busily darning his socks. Scrabbling about the woods hunting plant specimens, he even insisted one astonished youngster climb on his professor's back to reach a patch of lichen.

The exchange continued. More M.A.C. men followed Clark at Sapporo.

M.A.C.'s 1875 valedictorian, William Penn Brooks, arrived shortly after Clark's departure. "I have recently made a proposition that we have an agricultural fair here this fall," he wrote his sister in 1878. "I shall make it as much like a New England cattle-show as possible, omitting the 'hoss trot.'" Brooks married while on a visit home in 1882, and he and his wife, Eva, had two children in Sapporo. He spent twelve years there in all, four as college president.

As for Clark, he resigned from M.A.C. not long after returning to Amherst and entered into a partnership to found Clark & Bothwell, a silver-mining interest. Sadly, his partner proved to be something less than honorable, and after just two years in business, the company collapsed, taking with it Clark's reputation and the fortunes of numerous friends and family members. Paying the price with his health, he returned to Amherst, where he died in 1886.

But his unbowed likeness lives on in statues and murals around Hokkaido. And he'd brought something of Hokkaido—the specimens he gathered—home to Massachusetts. A century and a half later, dozens survive in the UMass herbarium. A couple of seeds Clark sent home in 1877 today provide greenery all year round in a corner of the campus Rhododendron Garden: two 60-foot examples of the majestic, slow-growing Japanese umbrella pine.

Sapporo Agricultural College, class of 1880, with William S. Clark and other professors from M.A.C. at center

Military exercises in front of South College, 1909

from the legislature to complete the college pond, supplying M.A.C. with "the one thing needful to make the landscape perfect—a water view."

The Massachusetts Agricultural College now had its iconic chapel and the pond that, generation after generation, would set the scene for memories of youth—of lolling on the grass, reveling in the first warm and fragrant days of spring. These two new features marked the terrain with evidence of M.A.C.'s rebirth—signs, as the twentieth century dawned, of its strength.

AN ESTABLISHED FACT

In the opening years of the new century, the college began to seem less like an experiment— that desolate "jumping off place" of 1867—and more like a steadily growing and improving educational institution.

When he was a trustee in the early 1890s, William Wheeler, class of '71, supervised construction of the campus pond.

By the end of the nineteenth century, the college had its chapel and pond, both symbolic of its resurgent strength. The drill hall built in 1883 is at left.

Chapel and Pond, M. A. C., Amherst, Mass.

Each autumn students descended from the trains in Amherst amid a profusion of trunks, and bolted for the electric cars that now connected nearby towns and carried passengers into the heart of campus. Soon—in 1911—a handsome "waiting station" would materialize on North Pleasant Street. Modern sewerage, electricity, and steam heating also made their appearances. Swamps had been drained, orchards, vineyards, and experimental plots coaxed into fruitfulness. Graceful elms, many planted by graduating classes, formed allées shading Olmsted Road, which made a semicircle with North Pleasant and gave access to the chapel and other main buildings. The experiment station answered thousands of letters each year. The library, once a source of particular embarrassment, now boasted more than 25,000 volumes, thanks largely to appeals by president and librarian Henry Goodell. And the zoological and botanical museums fairly bulged with the typical Victorian assortment of mounted and classified plants, taxidermied animals, eggs, shells, and such. Even the students looked different, clean-shaven (the heyday of voluminous burnsides having passed) and sophisticated.

In important respects they *were* different, reflecting an urbanizing and industrializing country and state. In 1905, though rural culture still held sway at M.A.C., about 40 percent of its students came from urban communities. A third were the sons of farmers, while 20 percent came from families of industrial wageworkers, and nearly half the students' parents earned their livings in small businesses or professional occupations.

They were more diverse in other ways, too. Among them were the first M.A.C. women; they would remain a small but determined minority until the 1920s. The first African-American students also had joined the student body by the turn of the century, even if a contemporary brochure exaggerated in speculating that M.A.C.'s founders would be amazed at how the college was "educating many of whom, at that early date, the country was fighting to free."

By 1905, moreover, the student body was some 250 strong and would continue to swell on a generous tide of full scholarships first voted on by the legislature in the 1880s.

Around the turn of the twentieth century, the approach to campus was along an elm-lined drive, with the new stone chapel in the distance.

Aggies were now far too numerous to cram into the double suites of South and North colleges (which by then rented for up to $18 a year, plus the cost of steam heat). Many had to take rooms in town, each abode transformed into "a mad arrangement of pictures, rugs, couches, desks, etc., with a smattering of old pipes" and perhaps "a stolen sign to fill some vacant spot."

All of these changes fed ambivalence among M.A.C. students about the "agricultural" label affixed to their college experience. Certainly it was disheartening to be seen as yokel farmer boys by students of the area's well-heeled private colleges, who had been known to refer to M.A.C. as the "cow college," its students "sod busters." M.A.C. students introducing themselves at Smith or Mount Holyoke would sometimes joke that they had to get up at 4 AM to join the early plow team; of course there was no plow team.

Indeed, some students and alumni found the Aggie label not only stigmatizing, but also misleading. Their college degrees often reflected scientific studies not necessarily

Cloudy with little rain. Wind northeast. Worked piling up manure in the yard. Have finished reading this evening Homer's Iliad.

This was a day in the life of 23-year-old Levi Stockbridge, recorded by the Hadley farmer himself on that damp day in 1843. As one whose family tree was deeply rooted in the Pioneer Valley—his ancestors helped settle the area in the seventeenth century—young Stockbridge represented a strong and colorful thread in the Yankee tradition.

He was opinionated, earnest, wry, well read, and worked like a mule. In his capacity as a state representative, as a perennial member of various agricultural societies, as farm superintendent, and later as professor of agriculture and president of Massachusetts Agricultural College, Stockbridge was always crafting passionate words in the service of a cause. "He believed a man was trained in some degree who could do any one thing well—hold a plow or make a plow," one of his students recalled. Stockbridge decried any arrangement smacking of Old World aristocracy, including railroad monopolies and undue concentrations of wealth.

And he believed in Massachusetts—believed in his neighbors, believed in the very dirt beneath his feet. "It is said our soil is sterile," Stockbridge posited in one of his many local addresses on agriculture. "Was it so originally? . . . Were the alluvial bottomlands of our valleys, of the Connecticut, the Housatonic, the Merrimac, and a score of others, the fine sweet loams of our foothills, sterile? It is impossible."

The Stockbridge House, built in 1728, was part of the old farm property the college trustees purchased before opening in 1867. Levi Stockbridge lived and worked there during his tenure at M.A.C. Today the building, the oldest house in Amherst, serves as the University Club.

geared toward practical agriculture. Entrance exams had become much more sophisticated and included subjects familiar in liberal arts colleges ("State briefly for what the following Romans are to be remembered: Coriolanus, Regulus, Cataline, Caesar, Mark Antony, Cicero, Nero."). In the early part of the twentieth century, students made a concerted effort to modify—sometimes even remove—the word *agricultural* when used in school publications and songs.

The young people of a burgeoning Commonwealth were eager for the broader offerings of a state college of arts and sciences. And in 1903 President Goodell took a modest step in that direction, organizing the school's first majors. Upperclassmen no longer had to follow a single course of study but could choose among six concentrations: agriculture, horticulture, biology, chemistry, math, and landscape gardening (a subject that would gain in depth and popularity under the newly hired professor of landscape architecture and botany, Frank A. Waugh). A faculty now numbering 20 professors and instructors was set to

In the age of urbanization and westward migration, Stockbridge wanted to prove that famers could stay in Massachusetts, restore its depleted soil, and prosper from abundant yields. During his first years at M.A.C. he developed the notion that it wasn't the soil's components one had to examine but those of the plant. Thus were hatched the so-called Stockbridge formulas, designed to supply the ground with precisely what a given crop—potatoes, say, or corn or asparagus—would take from the soil.

In 1876, Stockbridge began selling these fertilizers through the chemicals company launched by M.A.C. alumnus William H. Bowker ('71), under the proprietary name Stockbridge Special-Complete Manures. Though Stockbridge came under heavy criticism for patenting the formulas, he insisted it was only to prevent others from promoting fraudulent versions in an era teeming with impure or bogus miracle products. Bowker's company distributed the formulas freely, and anyone could buy ingredients like potash, nitrogen, and phosphoric acid. In any event Stockbridge gave his first royalties, amounting to $1,000, to the college.

"Feed the plant and the plant will feed you," urged the ads in farmers' journals. "There is no cheating the plant."

By the late 1880s, the Bowker Fertilizer Company had branches in New York City and Rochester, New York; Savannah, Georgia; Jacksonville, Florida; and Columbus, Ohio, with large factories in Elizabeth, New Jersey, and Brighton, Massachusetts.

"Ninety per cent of the best potatoes are now grown on the commercial fertilizers in place of stable manure," said a chemicals trade journal at the turn of the century, "and the Stockbridge leads, the sale of this brand running into thousands of tons each year."

Several years after Stockbridge's death in 1904, a Bowker ad in the *Country Gentleman* announced a contest for the largest yields grown on an acre of Stockbridge Corn Manure. The headline: "Who Says New England is Barren?"

William Bowker, class of '71, became a savvy, successful businessman who commercialized Stockbridge's best-selling manures.

teach a wider variety of courses, from livestock judging and market gardening to organic chemistry and entomology to constitutional history and English literature. In all majors, about a quarter of the students' time would be spent on the humanities and social sciences.

Another stride that distanced M.A.C. from its vocational roots: the advent of graduate-level work. In 1896 the "cow college" had produced its first two masters of science; in 1902 came the first doctorate, in entomology.

As if shucking off the nineteenth century itself, M.A.C. students of the twentieth

At a place called Ingleside just south of Holyoke, on a late-July afternoon in 1871, the Connecticut River was smooth as glass.

But a boisterous crowd of hundreds dotted the sandy banks, the span of the Chicopee Bridge, and the pleasant grounds of the Ingleside Inn. It was Regatta Week. Spectators included elegant ladies and working-class Irish boys. Crew teams from three colleges—Harvard, Brown, and the Massachusetts Agricultural College—all had their boosters. A bunch that had come in from Rhode Island on a horse-drawn omnibus sported brown veils and ribbons on their hats and lapels. The Harvard partisans wore magenta (which predated crimson as the school's color).

Betting was prodigious, with odds heavily favoring Harvard's experienced crew, which had competed at Oxford the year before. Brown was considered a contender. "Meanwhile," remarked Yale's college paper, "nobody thought anything about the chances of the Agriculturalists, except to smile good naturedly at the awkward appearance of the 40 or 50 hulking fellows who strolled about with big strips of maroon and white about their hats and 'M.A.C.' badges fastened to their waistcoats. . . . The Amherst College men call the students 'Aggies,' and yell 'Barn!' at them as an epithet of crushing contempt."

A correspondent for the *New York Times* talked with trainers of each crew before the race. "The Amherst Agriculturalists are a fine set of men, and their trainer, Josh Ward, is proud of them," he wrote. Ward explained that his boys had had only ten days' practice (which included walking to North Hadley and jogging back). Given these constraints, he'd decided "not to put the boys on severe training," instead giving them "coarse food and plenty of advice." They'd be competing in a boat used by Amherst the year before. However "hulking" the M.A.C. spectators may have appeared to Yale's correspondent, the heaviest of its six-man crew weighed in at 152 pounds.

After a long delay, at seven in the evening, finally the boats were in line.

And off they went, past the Ingleside, the Harvardians in the middle, the Agriculturalists beside the western bank. By the time the race approached the Chicopee Bridge, one shell had pulled away from the others and led by a considerable distance. "Harvard, of course," the spectators (according to the Yale *College Courant*) quickly concluded. "Hip her up, Harvard!" cried the magenta wearers (according to the *Times*).

century no longer were required to perform "chores" on the college farm. The many students of modest means, however, continued to vie for campus jobs waiting tables in the dining hall, oiling dormitory floors, or feeding animals in the veterinary lab. A member of the class of 1911 picked 140 quarts of strawberries in a morning to earn his train fare home one spring.

Unlike the labor rule, a requirement to appear at chapel would persist for decades; but already some chafed at that, too. As the student paper *Aggie Life* put it in 1899, "Compulsory chapel smacks too much of medievalism."

Seen here in 1870, the first year the school mounted a crew, four of these Aggies—Eldred, Allen, Leonard, and Simpson—returned in 1871, when they made school history by outstripping Harvard and Brown at that year's regatta.

But no, it was the white-shirted Agriculturalists. The crowd erupted as the Aggies shot under the bridge, a dozen lengths ahead, to finish in record time. "The men with the M.A.C. badges embraced one another and roared out some unearthly cheers and cries," said the *Courant*. "The Harvard and Brown men were dumb with astonishment and chagrin."

M.A.C.'s President Clark joyfully splashed into the water. There would be revelry in Amherst that night.

In truth, few who'd gathered at riverside that day could resist the thrill of this triumph by the underdog Aggies. Even a Brown man had to admit their stroke, while unscientific, had been powerful—"like death," he told the *Times*. "It was a fearful stroke," agreed a Harvard man, "but they made their old boat hum."

It seemed to the reporter that with every pull, the slight young Aggies had raised their boat "clean out of the water."

Pages from M.A.C.'s yearbook, *Index*, 1901–06

A FLOURISHING SOCIAL LIFE

The formal program at M.A.C. advanced no faster than faculty and administration thought wise. Student life, on the other hand, took off at a gallop. Countrified skating parties and modest receptions in the homes of faculty blossomed into a vivid and varied social calendar.

In her scrapbook of mementos, a M.A.C. class of 1907 woman carefully preserved a pocket-sized dance card for one of the early "informals" held in the college's plain but cavernous drill hall; the two-step went to Williams, the waltz was reserved for Whitaker, etc. These dances began in the afternoon, then broke for a catered meal, followed by more dancing and perhaps a bonfire and stroll across the moonlit campus. Finally, the visiting dates (mainly women) dashed to catch the trolley in time to satisfy their waiting chaperones. Junior and senior promenades were even splashier—gala evenings complete with engraved invitations and leather-bound programs.

Another student's keepsakes include an elegantly printed menu for the annual freshman banquet. The same young man kept mementos of a junior "smoker" (an informal get-together for men); a M.A.C. Spring Flower Show displaying expertly arranged corsages, wedding bouquets, and special-occasion gifts; a student vaudeville show; and a senior musical review. He'd seen the Boston Symphony play at Mass Aggie, caught a farce in three acts by the student drama club Roister Doisters, and seen the performance of a student-written musical comedy called "Pluto's Daughter."

In this period opportunities for musical expression could be found in the college glee club, choir, orchestra, and band. The newspaper of the 1890s, *Aggie Life*, became the *College Signal*, which in 1914 matured into that well-known fixture the *Massachusetts Collegian*.

The early years of the twentieth century also saw a flurry of fraternity organizing. Fraternities were nothing new at the school—its first, Kappa Tau Beta, or QTV, a home-grown M.A.C. organization, was established as early as 1869—but by 1910 founding of several new ones brought the total to ten. Two of the original secret societies now had their own houses and had expanded to become national organizations: Delta Gamma Kappa joined with Kappa Sigma and Phi Sigma Kappa planted additional chapters on campuses around the country. Obscure rituals and esoteric symbols of brotherhood were part of the fun; a yearbook from this period illustrates its entry on fraternities with a picture of skeletons in a graveyard clutching bottles and smokes. Through their newly formed Fraternity Conference, the fraternities also promoted the all-school dances and set rules for freshman rush.

Apart from a few shining moments such as M.A.C.'s upset victory in the crew regatta of 1871, sports at the college had for years been a modest affair, marked by intramural contests and casual schedules in which M.A.C. teams sometimes were matched against prep schools.

After the turn of the century, athletics became, on the contrary, the principal outlet for a surge in school spirit. The new rough-and-tumble sport of American football took center stage. Games were still played on an unleveled field between the stone chapel and drill hall, but beginning in 1901, M.A.C. alumni engaged a series of Dartmouth coaches to man the sidelines. These included Matthew Washington Bullock, who by joining M.A.C. in the fall of 1904 became the first black coach salaried by an integrated American college. After Bullock earned a law degree from Harvard in 1907, M.A.C. snapped him up for one more season. "We laugh at colleges our own size and rub it into colleges with twice our number," a college handbook from this period rousingly boasted. "We hold down or tie colleges many times our size, and best of all we are still coming."

The college also fielded competitors in basketball and track (with practice taking place in the drill hall), tennis (on two courts behind the drill hall), hockey (with the pond for a rink), and baseball.

Just as at most other colleges, good-natured rivalries among classes were part of M.A.C.'s college culture from the beginning, and they became more organized if not more heartfelt as the years passed. The usual dumping on freshmen included requiring them to wear beanies in the fall and proscribing them from donning corduroys or flannel shirts. For a while the student senate formed at the turn of the century even insisted the new-bies salute seniors and faculty members. A favorite prank was to dunk a freshman in the pond; another ritual involved disrupting the freshman banquet by capturing the class presi-dent. Student handbooks included instructions or "tips" for freshmen: "Do not strive to be amusing lest you encroach upon the province of the fool." Naturally the faculty frowned on the more reckless expressions of this rivalry, no less on the hooliganism that from time to time led to theft or destruction of school property. Students took an honor pledge explic-itly forsaking these behaviors.

Jack Ahern first encountered the beech trees between French Hall and the Durfee Conser-vatory when he was a UMass undergraduate in the early 1970s. An environmental design major, he was thrilled by their stature and by the smooth, silver-gray bark that gives the trees a strangely animal presence, "like something out of a fantasy world," he says.

The beeches greeted Ahern when he returned to campus in the 1980s to teach land-scape design, and they have remained, season after season, for more than a quarter-century.

"They are very beautiful in their maturity and old age," says Ahern. "They have long branches that reach down to the ground. There's a group of them there, that forms a rather intimate and special gathering."

The beeches are a living link to another age and to the man credited with planting at least two of the specimens, Samuel T. Maynard. Maynard arrived on the Amherst cam-pus as a student a century before Ahern—he graduated in 1872—and like Ahern, he soon returned to the college to teach horticulture and landscape design for the next 25 years.

Maynard was a great lover of trees as objects for study and things of beauty— "a most precious source of joy and comfort," as he wrote in 1899. He favored natural as opposed to formal, geometric groupings. "The trees we plant," Maynard wrote, "may be a legacy that will last through many generations."

It's a legacy transmitted not via names and dates but through shared aesthetic expe-rience. In a 2011 online survey inviting people to name their favorite places on the UMass campus, a number of respondents mentioned the old beech trees. Their comments follow a distinct theme, describing the grove as a place of soothing quiet and grace, a refuge from the stresses of university life.

FRESH DEDICATION TO COUNTRY LIFE

As M.A.C. was throwing out all these fresh shoots, a leader took over who would train its growth back toward rural concerns and occupations.

Arriving in 1906 as the new president, Kenyon L. Butterfield brought to M.A.C. the rural-life movement of which he was a prominent member. Just as progressive reformers of the day worked to free city dwellers from squalid, exploitative, and unhealthy conditions, Butterfield and others believed improved infrastructure and social institutions like schools, churches, and clubs could liberate rural folk from the isolation and drudgery that were hazards of country life. Butterfield, who had taught rural sociology at Michigan's agricultural college, envisioned a "new farmer" who would be adept at business, skilled in science, and richly cultured.

Indeed, M.A.C.'s most pressing concern, Butterfield thought, was "to clasp hands with the farmer himself." So in 1909 he initiated through a burst of outreach activities the college's extension service, including short summer and winter sessions for farmers; children's clubs; and traveling lectures, demonstrations, and exhibits by faculty and field agents

887 1888 1889 1890 1890 1891 1892 1893 1894 1895 1896 1897 1898 1899 1900 1901 1902 1903 1904 1905 1906 1907 1908 1909 1910 1911 1912 1

Just about every college campus has trees. Far fewer share UMass's designation as an arboretum—a collection of trees and shrubs curated for research and teaching value. And not many campuses are so richly endowed with ancient beauties that embody their institution's cultural heritage.

Beside South College, for example, is a tall, wide-spreading Japanese elm. Not only is it the first of its species to be grown in the United States, it also memorializes the sojourn in Japan of William Penn Brooks, an early graduate—and later, president—of Massachusetts Agricultural College, who brought the tree home in 1890. A classic old American elm commemorates the class of 1872, responsible for its planting, as well as the defunct landscape feature that it was part of—an elm-lined roadway. The spirit of 1908, a gargantuan pin oak, leafs out each spring beside Munson Hall.

The tradition in which departing students give a tree to their alma mater began with the college's very first graduating class of 1871. The practice ceased during and after World War II. Jack Ahern helped revive it in 1995 with that year's trident maple. It's an old tradition whose spirit could hardly be more forward looking. The class of 2011 planted a swamp white oak inaugurating what Ahern hopes will form a collection of class trees shading a walkway along the campus pond—a gift of joy and comfort to the UMass community of the twenty-second century.

The beech tree beside the Durfee Conservatory commemorates the class of 1910.

Different types of saddles, roadsters, and drafts being shown at a 1908 summer school demonstration (top). Summer sessions, part of President Butterfield's massive outreach initiative, offered short courses designed to attract farming men and women from nearby communities.

President-elect Kenyon L. Butterfield, ca. 1906

on everything from beekeeping to tree pruning. The local farmers' skepticism toward the college began to soften, and within a decade these extension programs had reached many thousands.

Butterfield also had a highly developed philosophy of teaching. He was fond of saying professors should teach *students* and not subjects, announcing themes like "balance" and "quality" for each academic year.

Perhaps even more importantly, he was expert at getting his message across to potential supporters. During the first 10 years of his administration, the college budget grew from roughly $150,000 to over $650,000.

Building accelerated. During the first decade of the twentieth century, four new academic buildings—Wilder, Clark, French, and Fernald Halls—were constructed across the campus pond from the chapel. Just north of the chapel another new cluster included a dining hall (Draper, built in 1903), dairy lab (Flint, 1912), and an agriculture building (Stockbridge, 1912).

Butterfield went hiring, too, seeking the country's best talent. In 1911 he oversaw a major academic restructuring, dividing 23 departments into five basic divisions: science; horticulture and landscape gardening; agriculture; humanities; and rural social science, a new subject area headed by Butterfield himself. These changes were accompanied by beefed-up offerings, especially in horticulture and agriculture. The latter division had two faculty in 1906; 10 years later 19 faculty taught agricultural courses, including new advanced classes in subjects like farm management and dairy science.

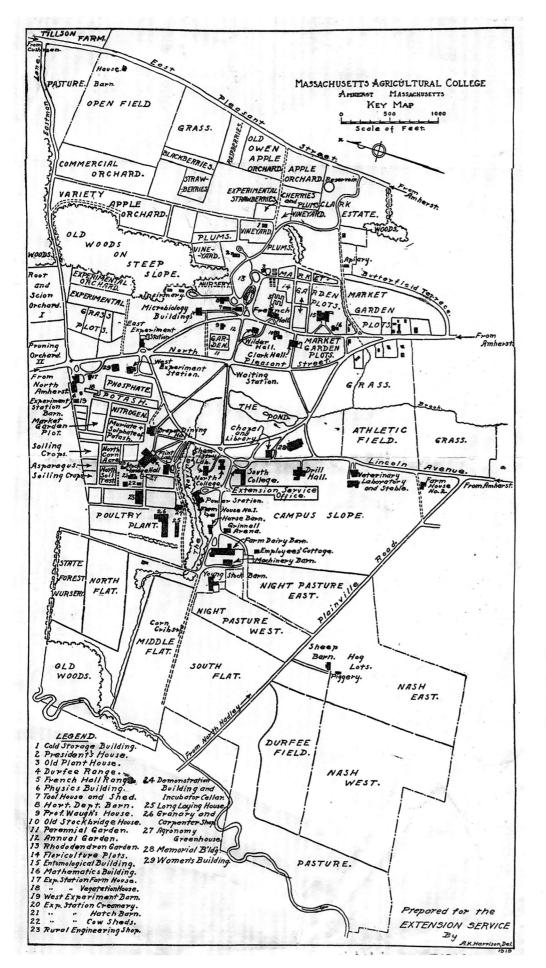

MASSACHUSETTS AGRICULTURAL COLLEGE
Amherst   Massachusetts
KEY MAP

0   500   1000
Scale of Feet.

LEGEND.
1 Cold Storage Building.
2 President's House.
3 Old Plant House.
4 Durfee Range.
5 French Hall Range.
6 Physics Building.
7 Tool House and Shed.
8 Hort. Dept. Barn.
9 Prof. Waugh's House.
10 Old Stockbridge House.
11 Perennial Garden.
12 Annual Garden.
13 Rhododendron Garden.
14 Floriculture Plots.
15 Entomological Building.
16 Mathematics Building.
17 Exp. Station Farm House.
18 "   "   Vegetation House.
19 West Experiment Barn.
20 Exp. Station Creamery.
21 "   "   Hatch Barn.
22 "   "   Cow Sheds.
23 Rural Engineering Shop.

24 Demonstration
     Building and
     Incubator Cellar.
25 Long Laying House.
26 Granary and
     Carpenter Shop.
27 Agronomy
     Greenhouse.
28 Memorial B'ld'g.
29 Women's Building.

Prepared for the
EXTENSION SERVICE
By
A.K.Harrison, Del.
1913

M.A.C. in 1913. After a half-century of development, the college farm had blossomed into an elaborate patchwork of orchards and experimental plots.

THE TOP WAVE

M.A.C. rounded its first half-century in full vigor. The college's first 50 years had seen the hard-fought establishment of three core enterprises—teaching, research, and outreach— that would endure into the twenty-first century. And it was truly a people's college. M.A.C. had flung open the doors of higher education to communities across the Commonwealth. Underlying all its activities had been a determination to seek prosperity for the country and especially for its New England home. These values would stand the test of time.

There's something about a body of water. It draws the eye, holds the attention, and over time becomes a repository of meaning.

The UMass campus pond is no exception. Within just a few years of its establishment in the winter of 1892, this feature had become the undisputed focal point of what was then Massachusetts Agricultural College. "From the entrance of the driveway there is a delightful view of the campus and college buildings," said a college promotional pamphlet in 1898. "In the foreground there is a small pond with its wooded island, across which can be seen the chapel and the two large dormitories."

Developing the pond was the work of many. Two students took the initiative in the winter of 1891 to dam up Tan Brook, the stream that meandered through campus on its way to the Mill River. Evidently the effect was pleasing. In June 1892 the college trustees voted to make the dam and pond permanent, assigning alumnus William Wheeler of M.A.C.'s first graduating class to supervise the work. President Henry Goodell went to the legislature for an appropriation of $1,000. The job was largely complete by January 1893, although Wheeler reported that additional funds would be required to correct errors in levels made by the student workers.

The pond's builders clearly intended it to be ornamental, the water feature needed to complete any gracious Victorian landscape garden. In early years it also served a practical function, providing ice for cold storage of dairy and fruit products.

For more than a century the pond has been a magnet for student life. After 1909 it provided a dramatic snowbound setting for hockey games. Also around this time, the pond played a key part in the traditional rivalry between classes and hazing of freshmen. "Pond party" was the name given to a ritual in which upperclassmen marched a young man down to its marshy banks and tossed him in. For more than 50 years, the annual spring rope pull across the pond matched freshmen against sophomores in 60-man teams stationed on opposite banks. Families from the surrounding countryside came to watch the excitement and take part in the merriment when one team gave way and went tumbling into the drink.

Later in the twentieth century the pond became the scene of elaborate snow sculptures in the annual Winter Carnival. For years, spring pop concerts featuring headliners

But challenges also lay ahead. No one understood that better than those who had given their lifeblood to the college when its very survival was at stake. William Bowker was the freshman who felt he'd reached "the jumping off place" when he arrived on campus in 1867. More than 40 years later, a loyal alumnus and highly successful manufacturer of farm chemicals, Bowker sat down to write President Butterfield. "We are on the top wave of popularity," he wrote, referring to an especially generous state appropriation, "and on that account we have grave responsibilities as well as dangers."

1901 1902 1903 1904 1905 1906 1907 1908 1909 1910 1911 1912 1913 1914 1915 1916 1917 1918 1919 1920 1921 1922 1923 1924 1925 1926 1927 19

A "pond party," early twentieth century

from Bob Dylan to Queen Latifah and Jazz in July performances drew audiences to the pond's edge. The campus pond lawn has hosted protests, pep rallies, sack races, egg tosses, juggling, skydiving exhibitions, Frisbee, and, in 1987, a record-breaking Twister game involving more than four thousand participants. In the 1970s, one guy tried to jump its muddy waters on a bike; 30 years later another student just rode right in with a splash— and, naturally, posted the video on YouTube.

For many tens of thousands of students over the years, the pond's most important role has been as the lovely natural backdrop for daily life on campus, a scene that came to represent the UMass experience itself.

"I will never forget the way the moon looked so surreal against the shimmering waters of the pond next to the modern library and the ancient chapel," one alumna wrote to *UMass Magazine* in 2001. "If I studied late, sometimes I would stroll by there in the dead of winter and not hear a sound. . . . On a sunny day, students [would be] strewn about sunning themselves or reading a book for class or just plain staring at the world because they were so glad winter had come and gone."

1914 *College Signal* becomes
Massachusetts Collegian

1915 First game on Alumni Field

1916 Mount Toby purchased for $30,000

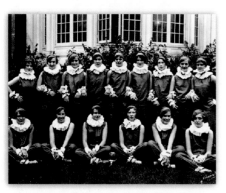

- First sorority, Delta Phi Gamma, established

1917 To bolster war effort, faculty votes to give
students credit for 12 weeks of farm work

1918 State dissolves college charter, making M.A.C.
a state agency

- Butterfield adds electives in food and clothing
preparation, home management, and nursing

1919 M.A.C. holds memorial service for
community's 51 war dead

1920 Abigail Adams House, first women's
dorm, built

- Memorial Hall dedicated

1923 Waltham land received as gift

1924 Edward M. Lewis replaces Butterfield

1926 Tuition for Massachusetts
residents = $60

1927 Roscoe M. Thatcher replaces Lewis

1931 M.A.C. becomes Massachusetts State College
(M.S.C.)

- Curry Hicks
Physical Educa-
tion Building
constructed

1933 Shortage of space for women denies
consideration for 70

- Tuition = $100

- Hugh Potter
Baker succeeds
Thatcher as
president

1935 Massachusetts Federation of Labor successfully lobbies for engineering department

- Economics department established

- Goodell Library opens

1938 B.A. degree established

1939 Massachusetts State College Building Association incorporated

1941 Enrollment = 1,263 students; World War II reduces number to 725 by 1944

1944 G.I. Bill passes

1945 Enrollment climbs back to 1,002

1946 1,300 veterans enter Fort Devens campus

1947 Legislation establishes M.S.C. as University of Massachusetts

- School of Engineering founded

1948 Sports teams dubbed the Redmen

- Ralph Van Meter becomes president

1949 Fort Devens campus closes

1950 School of Business Administration founded

1951 *Massachusetts Quarterly* established

1953 School of Nursing founded

1954 Jean Paul Mather takes over presidency

1955 Sciences and liberal arts joined to create College of Arts and Sciences

1956 School of Education founded

- "Freedom bill" allows faculty members to receive salary incentives

1957 Student Union Building constructed

1959 *Massachusetts Review* founded

- Public Health Center constructed

1960 John W. Lederle succeeds Mather as president

1962 State grants trustees greater fiscal autonomy

1963 Centennial celebration (enrollment = 7,600, an all-time high)

Mass! Mass! Mass'chusetts!
Rah! Rah! Rah! Rah!

—Twentieth-century cheer

BIRTH OF A UNIVERSITY

From Mass Aggie to UMass

BY THE EARLY TWENTIETH CENTURY, THE STONE CHAPEL OF THE MASSACHUSETTS AGRICULTURAL COLLEGE PRESIDED WITH AN AIR OF PERMANENCE OVER ITS PASTORAL CAMPUS. THE RHYTHMS OF COLLEGE LIFE — THE COMINGS AND GOINGS OF STUDENTS, THE ROUNDS OF DANCES AND EXAMINATIONS — SEEMED AS INEVITABLE AS THE SEASONS. M.A.C. HAD SECURED A PLACE FOR ITSELF AMONG THE PEOPLE OF THE COMMONWEALTH.

But just what role the college should play as a state institution of higher learning was a question only provisionally answered in the first 50 years of its history. Should its emphasis be vocational? And if so, should the state college prepare young men to take up agricultural pursuits, or should it train them for roles in the industrial world whose mills and factories now had their place even in a sleepy town like Amherst? For that matter, why shouldn't young citizens of modest means enjoy access to the kind of education offered at private colleges—the kind that would suit them for the professions and enlarge their lives with a knowledge of literature, history, and philosophy?

The lights of old South
    College one by one
Blossom in fire; across the
    quiet Pond
A murmur stirs and
    whispers and is gone.
The North Star shines on
    Toby; and beyond
The sorrow and the
    heartache and the scars
Wheel the inviolable
    squadrons of the stars.

—From a poem by
    Willard Wattles
    (M.A.C. instructor),
    ca. 1917

Robert H. Chapon, first M.A.C. student
killed in action in World War I

These questions would dominate the college's second 50 years. If the great challenge of M.A.C.'s first half-century was a fight for survival, the struggle of the second half-century was to finally establish its identity.

During this process, the state college also was responding to the exigencies of a difficult age. The institution that emerged as the University of Massachusetts in 1947 forged this identity in the crucible of two world wars, a global depression, and enormous changes in American society. This period saw the rise of a great American middle class that pushed for access to higher education as the path to a fuller and more prosperous life—fulfilling the dream, really, of M.A.C.'s fire-breathing republican founders. The first part of the twentieth century also brought the enfranchisement and emancipation of women; as young citizens of the Commonwealth, in greater and greater numbers, they, too, arrived at North Pleasant Street to stake their claim on the riches of higher learning.

WAR

M.A.C. was in the midst of robust growth as well as a resurgent embrace of ruralism inspired by President Kenyon L. Butterfield when, in the summer of 1914, word reached campus that the world's great powers were embarking upon a fearsome and violent clash. The first M.A.C. student to take the call to arms in World War I, Robert Henri Chapon, had graduated that spring. He returned to his home country, France, and enlisted in its army. Before the year was out, he died in battle near Verdun.

Chapon was one of several M.A.C. students to enlist in foreign military service prior to the entry of the United States into the war. Another notable example was Frederick Vail Waugh, son of Frank Waugh, the college's renowned professor of landscape architecture and botany. Students at Amherst College joined those at M.A.C. to raise ambulance unit SSU 539 to serve the French cause. It remained in service and was later switched to aid U.S. troops once this country joined the fray.

The great majority of members of the M.A.C. community remained on this side of the Atlantic, where the war seemed to be taking place at a great distance, but the struggle seemed critical to many of them nevertheless, for they saw Germany's depredations as an attack on enlightened ideals that stood at the heart of both America and the college itself. "The Hun aims—blindly, perhaps, but surely and inevitably—to re-establish some of the old world's outworn and impossible arrangements and institutions," wrote Dean (and later, president) Edward M. Lewis. "For the light as we see it, he is bound to substitute his light; the old tyranny for our new liberty."

After the U.S. officially entered the war in April 1917, the campus began to empty of students. Within weeks the faculty voted to give credit for 12 weeks of farm work, an attempt to bolster the war effort by replacing agricultural workers lost to the military and boosting the food supply to feed civilians, U.S. fighting men, and desperate Allies abroad. Students left campus early and fanned out to the countryside in droves.

In May an Officers Training School opened at Plattsburgh, New York, drawing off 43 M.A.C. men, most of whom ultimately went to war. By June 1, nearly all of M.A.C.'s five hundred students were performing emergency war service, most in agriculture, about

10 percent in the military. A second officers training session began at Plattsburgh in August, and a third opened at Yaphank, Long Island, in January 1918.

That month, Lieutenant Louis W. Ross, M.A.C. class of 1917, wrote home describing what his men endured on a 90-mile march across a snowy French countryside. "At night," he wrote, "having nothing but barns to stop in, their shoes would freeze hard, and it was necessary to burn straw in them in order to get them on again, and then some would burn the soles out, thereby necessitating walking in practically bare feet—they had to do it." By the spring of 1918 many more students and alumni had enlisted or been drafted, sons of Massachusetts who would know trenches, poison gas, and machine-gun fire.

Back in Amherst, sports had been suspended as America entered the war, then partially reinstated, then suspended again. The *Collegian* continued to publish, with a special supplement the summer of 1917 for men in the field. That November, a campus committee assembled Christmas boxes for M.A.C. boys overseas, and to those in U.S. camps, it sent coupons for admission to camp theaters.

M.A.C. faculty and extension staff threw themselves behind the food-supply cause, much of the work under the auspices of the state Committee on Food Production, which Butterfield headed. They gave lectures and demonstrations on food conservation, preservation, and production; supervised the planting and harvesting of gardens by Massachusetts children; conducted research on canning, soy beans, and the protein needs of young animals; and published dozens of circulars and bulletins.

After a staggering death toll in the tens of millions, at last an armistice came in November 1918. Students returned in large numbers during the spring and fall of 1919, including hundreds of disabled veterans, seeking training in agriculture under a federal program. That spring, Dean Lewis, acting as president while Butterfield was in Europe helping to supervise education for troops interested in farming on return to civilian life, held a memorial service at Mass Aggie. The families of 17 of the community's 51 dead took what solace they could from Bach's solemn Prelude and Fugue in G.

The college's war record was a source of anguish but also of enormous pride—and a new unity. That much was clear one night in late October 1919—World Aggie Night—when M.A.C. men in 25 cities pledged nearly $150,000 to erect perhaps the campus's finest building to date: Memorial Hall. Dedicated in 1921, it was the first such commemorative building on any American campus. Generations of youth in their daily rounds would pass before the classical pillars and wooden moldings that seem to hold aloft the inscription, "We will keep faith with you who lie asleep."

STATE CONTROL

At the scaled-down commencement exercise of 1917, Butterfield urged the class to remember that life, with all its challenges, would resume after the war. "New problems will arise," he said, "that have never come up before in quite the same fashion."

All too true, as it turned out. That the government in Boston had taken ownership of the college was a mixed blessing. It meant support and credibility but also placed on the college the burden of serving state constituencies whose goals sometimes conflicted, or

For 50 years, students and alumni of Mass Aggie lamented the lack of a decent athletic field on campus. Sure, they mounted baseball and football games on a couple of acres just west of the stone chapel. But there was no room for bleachers or a ticket gate. The ground was lumpy. A long pitch could get lost among the maples.

This was hardly the sort of facility a scrappy ag college needed to win the respect of its well-heeled rivals. In fact, M.A.C. frequently was confined to playing against high schools and small colleges because of its inability to host a high-stakes contest on home turf.

Proud alumni attempted to raise funds to construct a good field in the 1890s and again in 1902. These efforts ran aground partly because of economic hard times but also because the faculty and administration were none too enthusiastic about college sports, which many saw as often brutish, rife with ethical problems like favoritism for athletes, and in general a colossal distraction from the educational task at hand. As late as 1929 college debaters took on the question of whether to abolish intercollegiate sports altogether, with that position's interlocutor saying such programs "injure participants physically and scholastically."

Before the construction of Alumni Field, football and other sports were played on a few acres located next to the stone chapel (top).

"Athletics for all" on Alumni Field (bottom), ca. 1940

These divergent perspectives on the role of athletics at M.A.C. were largely resolved in the person of Curry S. Hicks. Hired by President Butterfield while still in his twenties, Hicks came to M.A.C. in 1911 full of ideas about physical education and the reform of college sports.

For one thing, he thought that drill-hall calisthenics and military maneuvers, long the mainstay of physical education at the college, should indeed be replaced by actual athletic competitions—games. Yet Hicks also argued that the purpose of athletics wasn't school publicity or even sport per se, but the physical development of each student. "Athletics for all," including and perhaps especially for the physically underdeveloped student, was his goal. Finally, upon his hiring, Hicks insisted that all varsity coaches should be full-time teaching staff, not people hired by the season whose jobs depended on winning alone.

Within months of Hicks's arrival, the college created a committee to supervise athletics consisting of student team managers, alumni, faculty, and the president. In 1913 a renewed and united campaign was launched to raise money to create a bona fide athletic field on boggy land just east of Lincoln Avenue. Hicks himself was at the center of the effort, traveling to alumni clubs around the country to make his pitch.

Students did their part, too, as noted in the *Collegian* (February 2, 1915):

> Once more the Athletic Field campaign reached a point where immediate financial assistance was necessary, and once more the student body, almost to a man, rose to the occasion, responding royally to the needs of the field. In all, a little over $1,000 was pledged by the undergraduates. . . . The students have clearly shown that they want the field both by moral and financial support. The juniors sacrificed their annual banquet, one of the biggest affairs of their college life, in order to turn money over to the field.

The class of 1917 contributed 25 tons of lime and four tons of fertilizer. Students also contributed hundreds of hours of labor, grading, laying tile drains, and seeding the field. The class of 1903 assumed responsibility for building an entrance gate.

In the spring of 1915, still pressing for bleachers, a quarter-mile cinder track, and a sturdy fence, alumnus C. A. Peters ('97) penned a *Collegian* appeal to his fellow alumni, turning aside excuses for not doing more. "One man says, 'I supposed every one in our class had given but me'; another, 'Our class secretary is as good as dead.' . . . This is the first object of any size that the alumni have been called on to support and it is time the call was answered. Shake up your class secretary. Raise the money yourself. Get the old missionary spirit. Did the old college do anything for you?"

Curry S. Hicks shoveling the hockey rink

This all-out fundraising approach would come around again in the late 1920s when the college community worked toward its first serious gymnasium with a pool and an indoor track—the Curry Hicks Cage. "Contributions are coming in so fast these days that definite figures concerning the status of the campaign are about impossible to get," said the *Collegian* in late 1929. Alumni, students, and friends of the college gave tens of thousands to the project.

As for Alumni Field, it would be the site of many a home game. The first came in October 1915 with a victory over Colby College.

The following year, the college handbook declared a more general victory. "During the last few years Aggie has become very prominent in the athletic world. . . . She is now being asked for dates by the largest and best known colleges. The new athletic field has added greatly to the success of her teams and will add more."

Of course, pride and student investment in the field meant yet another onerous duty for newbies: "It is a college tradition," announced a 1920s student handbook, "that all freshmen shall do their bit when asked to perform any labor necessary to keep the Alumni Field in good condition. Remember that every bit of labor when the field was built, was done by the students themselves."

Memorial Hall (right); World War I—era bayonet drills (inset)

simply changed. It seemed some group was always investigating college operations—the state Ways and Means Committee in 1911, the state Commission on Economy and Efficiency in 1913, a special commission on agricultural education in 1918, the Massachusetts Farm Bureau Federation in 1921, among others. All were interested in what the college was doing, or should be doing, with state dollars.

In 1918, as part of an overall effort to systematize state administration, the issue of control reached a head. The state dissolved the college's charter and made it a state agency, placing it under the department of education, subject to state oversight of everything from salaries to publications.

After the stirring return of its veterans, M.A.C. entered a dispiriting period of declining enrollment and faculty turnover. The agrarian boom Butterfield had so passionately espoused was over. And state control could sometimes feel like a stranglehold, especially to administrators like Butterfield who had accomplished so much at the college. The director of the experiment station, for example, complained that a request for $4 emergency travel money had to pass through the college president and three or four state entities and that state supervisors often held experiment station bulletins until they were out of date.

College leaders energetically sought to overturn the new arrangement, but in vain. In 1924, Butterfield resigned in frustration. "For nearly five years," he wrote, "I have been compelled to work under a system of state house control which, as applied to the College, I regard as wholly unsound in principle, in practice highly detrimental to efficiency and true economy, as well as seriously discouraging to my co-workers on the staff."

Dean Lewis took up the presidency, but by the spring of 1927, he, too, was ready to throw in the towel. "I have seen my judgments and recommendations as an executive overturned or set aside," he wrote in an annual report.

WOMEN STAKE THEIR CLAIM

If administrators saw the war and its aftermath as a time of depletion for the college, for women at M.A.C. these years were, to the contrary, a period of exhilarating expansion into new realms. During the academic year 1912–13 there were five women at the college; by 1917–18 there were 30, and that number doubled by 1920. Mae Holden Wheeler '16 recalled her early college years: "Everything was taken care of as far as our studies were concerned, but we were more or less overlooked. As the number of girls increased, I think they began to make themselves felt in the college."

Amid liberalizing attitudes about women's rights and abilities, the war had ushered in special opportunities—a need for women's labor and expertise in such areas as home management, gardening, and food preservation and conservation. Women students moved into emptied M.A.C. fraternity houses; they left campus to do war work on nearby farms just like the men. As a 1918 annual report put it, "This very emergency that is reducing our attendance of men increases the call for special work for women."

While the college had long tolerated women's attendance, it had done next to nothing to encourage or support it. But in 1918 Butterfield asked for an appropriation to begin a women's program. The next year, M.A.C. launched new electives in food and clothing preparation, home management, and nursing. Edna Skinner came on to serve as women's advisor and to head the new Rural Home Life department, and Adeline Hicks launched a program in women's recreation and gymnastics (her husband, Curry S. Hicks, had been teaching physical education to men since 1911).

After the 1916 acquisition of a "demonstration forest" of more than 700 acres on Mt. Toby, the college held an annual Mountain Day highlighted by outdoor festivities and refreshments.

Female students had traditionally bunked in Draper (the dining hall) or stayed in town; now work began on a Georgian Revival women's dorm west of North Pleasant Street. To find a fitting name for the new accommodation, the college announced a contest open to "Massachusetts girls." Soon a letter arrived from 14-year-old Katherine Ehnes of Medfield, who'd done club work since the age of 11 and won an honorable mention in canning. Abigail Adams, she wrote, had "controlled the affairs of the household and farm" while her husband was away, a "true mother of the Revolution." Abigail Adams House opened in 1920, the very year American women won the vote.

Women plunged into student life. While M.A.C. men in the 1920s focused, frankly, on hazing younger students—the "night-shirt parade," in which freshmen were herded outdoors, set upon, and stripped of their pajamas, had its heyday—the far less numerous women drew together for support. In 1916 they founded the first sorority, Delta Phi Gamma, to "promote a feeling of unity and a stronger friendship among the girls of the college." The handful of women faculty members joined, too. Several more sororities followed in the 1930s. The women's student government, formed in 1919, not only enforced rules but also held teas and "assist[ed] the freshmen to make their adjustment to the college environment."

Women joined the Landscape Art Club, the Florist and Gardeners Club, the women's glee club, and the women's orchestra; they took up roles on the *Collegian* and college yearbook, the *Index*. The drama club Roister Doisters, which had assigned female roles to men, cast actual women in the 1920s; in 1931, a woman became president of the organization. In 1933 a women's debating team got under way; that same year, the six women of the Outing Club enjoyed, along with nine men, a 35-mile hike across the Holyoke Range, around Mt. Warner, over Sugarloaf, to the top of Mt. Toby and back down again.

As much as women transformed college culture, they also were kept separate. Female faculty were paid less than men. Women students led lives regimented by an array of paternalistic rules that didn't apply to men. "Each Freshman may keep her light burning after 11:00 PM as long as she may desire six times a term," read a 1925 women's handbook. "Each 'sit-up' shall be reported on the floor bulletin board." Women could go to movies in town only in groups of three including an upper-class student and had to wear long coats over riding breeches or bloomers when riding trolleys. They had to be in the dorm at 6:30 PM in winter, 7:30 in spring and fall. A 1930s women's handbook, quoting Shakespeare, admonished, "If I lose mine honor, I lose myself."

Women's athletics, 1920s

AMID HARD TIMES, A PUSH FOR OPPORTUNITY

In the late 1920s, enthusiasm and overall demand for the college's offerings began rising again; unprecedented numbers of young people came knocking on M.A.C.'s doors. But another historic disaster—the Great Depression—soon fell like a hammer blow across the country. Would-be collegians increasingly faced financial straits that prevented them from enrolling.

Stagnating appropriations for instruction and facilities forced the college to stem enrollment increases. In the fall of 1933, student numbers were up 20 percent, but the college had closed enrollment to women in July because there was no place to house them; 70 candidates were refused consideration. In his 1933 report, new college president Hugh Potter Baker remarked that this flood of applicants was made up of young people "who, under normal circumstances, might go to more expensive institutions." They in turn were "taking the places of the poorer boys and girls who have to give up the opportunity entirely." Not only women but also African-Americans and the children of Polish, Jewish, and Italian immigrants were increasingly looking to the college for a way into the American Dream. "They have had so little done for them that they come to us unspoiled and are usually appreciative of every favor," remarked a 1933 faculty study on curriculum goals. "On our shoulders rests the responsibility for their development."

By 1926 tuition for Massachusetts residents was $60, and it rose to $100 by 1933. Scholarships, all but nonexistent in the first years of the Depression, then flowed at a trickle in the form of campus jobs and "only to worthy students of high character, whose habits of life are economical and who have maintained an average of at least 70%." A pamphlet on women students in 1933 reported that most were struggling to stay on and appealed for donations of used clothing. "The feeling of well-being which comes from comfortable clothing and the right thing to wear has been secured for a number of students," it said.

During the 1920s and 1930s, the old questions about curriculum increasingly became an issue of access. As other states expanded the roles of land-grant colleges and universities, industrial workers and labor unions of the Commonwealth pressed for similar low-cost options in Massachusetts—whether on the Amherst campus or elsewhere. Though some held fast to the Aggie traditions, favoring vocational and scientific offerings, other young people across the state clamored for an affordable college of arts and sciences, and still others argued for a full-scale university complete with professional schools.

In the fall of 1927, President Roscoe Thatcher broke with M.A.C. tradition by donning academic cap and gown for his inaugural address—"not," he explained, "from any personal preference for this picturesque garb," but to represent "the standards and quality of academic work which should prevail at the College." Indeed, during the 1920s administrators approved modest additions to the course of study, beefing up government, history, and economics offerings, some of which found their way into the required core curriculum. The change of name of the Horticultural Manufactures department to Food Sciences was telling, as was the institution of the Home Economics department in 1924.

But by the fall of 1928, students on campus felt the time for small measures had come and gone. They wanted their degrees to bear the name Massachusetts State

College—reflecting the broad nature of their studies (only 30 percent of upperclassmen majored in agricultural subjects) and carrying the prestige of any non-vocational college degree. A group calling itself the Agitation Committee adopted the rather sophisticated strategy of taking its message to the Massachusetts public, which also had been agitating

Helen Curtis early in her career at UMass Amherst

As the first full-time dean of women at UMass—and for many years virtually the only female voice in policy debates—Helen Curtis had an enormously complex job on her hands.

Hired in 1945, just as World War II vets began claiming the education that was their due, Curtis's task was to ease the way for the women students who, frankly, ranked low among the institution's priorities. Her other job was to fight, patiently but insistently, to change these priorities and win for university women the equal footing that was *their* due as citizens of the Commonwealth.

A variously gifted person, this woman hailing from a small town in South Dakota was well suited to the challenge. To the students she guided, Curtis was accessible, understanding, a keeper of confidences, and a ready source of encouragement. As an administrator she was tactful and politically astute but fearless in pressing a just cause. Helen Curtis, a rather small woman favoring demure suits, had the heart of a lion.

Curtis concerned herself with virtually every aspect of women's college experiences. She encouraged them to follow their inclinations into male-dominated fields (even if those fields were not eager to welcome them). She helped them get the financial support they needed to continue their educations. She addressed herself to uniquely female social and personal issues.

Among Curtis's contributions was establishment of a system of student "house counselors" in the women's dorms. "[W]e tried to have girls with different religions, different interests, some independents, some sorority girls—all people who really wanted to help new students," said Curtis in a 1976 interview. "They were outstanding girls who really coveted the role as one of honor and service." She also started a summer counseling program to help orient freshmen. Curtis supported the dorm closing hours and other regulations for women as sometimes (in her words) "picayune" but overall designed to ensure security and promote an environment conducive to study.

When the School of Engineering opened in 1947, some of the university's most ambitious students flocked to the discipline for its promise of a prosperous career in a burgeoning industry. "Women were interested in it," recalled Curtis. "Faculty advisors tried to steer them away from it as they thought women couldn't handle such difficult courses. There was really a reluctance to admit women in engineering, animal husbandry, pre-med, and the School of Business. But some women persisted and proved they could handle such majors very well."

Nearly 30 years later, she recalled them individually. There was the female student who hit it out of the park in electrical engineering, graduating with honors. One woman

for new options in higher education. On October 2, 1929, the *Collegian* reported that President Thatcher wanted to await a federal report on land-grant colleges. He valued the Aggie name for its "historical significance." But the student committee "want[ed] to have the name of the College changed immediately" and was "carrying on agitation . . . to let

concentrating in mechanical engineering became an officer of the Engineering Society. A brilliant female economics major won a coveted fellowship and went on to an illustrious career in the federal government. Curtis had believed in these pioneering young women, fought for them, and shares credit for their success.

In addition to supporting honor societies and sororities for regular students, Curtis found herself serving as a sounding board and helper to older, returning female students whose concerns were quite different. "Some of them were girls who had dropped out as sophomores or juniors, or dropped out to marry or have babies," she recalled. "Later, they realized that they had problems, and they needed as much education as they could get in order to cope with their lives alone. A lot of them were really successful." Often they had children to support and husbands who'd walked out. Curtis and a colleague, Margaret Hamlin, started an emergency fund for these situations. "Sometimes," said Curtis, "it was just fifteen dollars if a girl had broken her glasses, or bus fare home for a weekend if she was worried about her mother who'd gone to the hospital."

All the while Curtis was serving—often as the sole woman—on various university committees, in particular pushing for gender equity in admissions, financial aid, and faculty appointments, all of which then favored men. At times it was a lonely task. "I think at first many of the men were skeptical about having a woman on committee," she said.

If thwarted in her advocacy for too long, the mild-mannered Curtis was fully capable of directing a "blast"—as she described it in 1969—toward the powers that be. The policy on faculty, she wrote, "has been to consider men only for positions of rank and to exploit the availability of wives of staff for support staff with lower rank and lower pay."

By the early 1970s, of course, Curtis's arguments were backed by the force of federal nondiscrimination law. She saw this as a critical ingredient in the progress that followed. "My methods of 'persuasion,'" she remarked, "were useful in their time but not *enough*."

And yet what Curtis gave UMass for 28 years *was* enough; it was more than enough. As the institution's gadfly, she was its most devoted friend. "Change! Change!" she cried in 1976. "It *is* a great university on the way to becoming a greater one."

Dean Curtis was lionized in the spring 1992 issue of *Massachusetts*.

The automobile made its appearance on campus—and almost everywhere—in the early twentieth century. By midcentury the need for parking had become substantial.

the public know" that the students intended to pursue their cause until they achieved this goal. Alumni generally supported the change, though debate was fierce. Philip F. Whitmore '15, for example, wrote the *Collegian* saying he took offense at the students' "hostility to the term 'agricultural.'"

In the end, the timing of the college's name-change had as much to do with pressure from without as from within. A proposed state referendum to found a state college in Boston that might prove a formidable rival to M.A.C. sent the trustees scrambling to present the legislature with their own request for that status; on April 15, 1931, the state made it so. After nearly a century of fitful progress as an Aggie, the state's institution of higher learning finally took on the proud name of Massachusetts State College (M.S.C.).

This move by no means ended debate about college offerings. In 1934 the alumni voted their approval for awarding bachelor of arts degrees. Once again administrators hesitated, Dean William L. Machmer expressing the apprehension that a move toward the traditionally more patrician enterprise of liberal arts education would lead to "competing camps" at the school and a decline in enrollment by the working people the college was pledged to serve.

The forces of change were reaching critical mass, however. In 1935 the Massachusetts Federation of Labor lobbied successfully for the establishment of an engineering department at the college. A separate economics department was established the same year. In 1938 the trustees established the bachelor of arts degree, adding the B.A. to the bachelor of science, bachelor of landscape art, and bachelor of vocational agriculture already offered. M.S.C. renamed its Division of Social Sciences—which had included such subjects as literature and fine arts—the Division of Liberal Arts. About that time the music department also was founded.

Still unsatisfied, the people of the Commonwealth pressed their case for a full-fledged university. Again various constituencies put forward proposals to attach the name to other institutions; the *Collegian* adopted a masthead motto, "Graduate from U. of M." In 1941, a hearing on a bill proposing a second name-change for the college found proponents arguing that 20,000 Massachusetts youth were being educated out of state and wanted their own university.

Before this matter could come to fruition, however, the people of Massachusetts were forced to turn their attention to graver concerns. The country was again at war.

WORLD WAR II AND ITS AFTERMATH

Weeks after Germany invaded Poland in September 1939, Massachusetts State College students over the age of 18 filed into Memorial Hall to register for the draft. After spring vacation 1941, a voluntary physical training program for national defense began, and soon the exodus of male students got under way in earnest.

But this time M.S.C. continued to operate more or less at full tilt—as a predominately female college and military training site. Extension agents once again took up the job of promoting food production and conservation, but academic schedules continued with relatively few interruptions. The total number of students in regular programs stood at 1,263 in 1941. It dropped to 725 by 1944; fully six hundred of these students were women.

Meanwhile, the campus became a place to gather and train young men for war. In March 1943 the 58th College Training Detachment of the Army Air Force brought seven hundred trainees to campus for classes in math, physics, English, and history; ultimately 2,380 cadets received this preparation. A Reserve Officers' Training Corps (ROTC) briefly attended classes on the Amherst campus, followed by a group of pre-draft, 17-year-old Air Corps Reservists receiving a basic first-year course.

In July 1943 Dean Machmer wrote to a former student stationed in a military malaria survey unit on the West Coast:

> Could you be in my office today and look over the campus, you would view a sight which is heartening. It is peaceful, beautiful, and, yet, in step with the difficult times through which we are passing. There are the quiet pond, the close cut deep green lawns, the stately trees and the well swept walks and drives. Never has the campus been more beautiful. But as you look there appear bevies of care-free, yet serious, summer session students. Mingled among them [are] hundreds of pre-flight trainees in uniform marching to and from their scheduled assignments. Yes, there is a military air here, but we shall continue to carry on a full college program for our civilian students. It is certain that our enrollment will have relatively few men students, but the number of women students will be larger than ever, and they are really a select group of college women. We feel proud of them.

Ironically, perhaps, it wasn't the war itself so much as its aftermath that would dramatically transform the college, ultimately replacing the pastoral air of its swept walks and green lawns with the swarming activity of a densely developed town—and sealing its identity as the University of Massachusetts.

INDEX 1935

Page Two Hundred Fifty-two

A stylish 1930s yearbook montage suggests the diversification of the school's activities and the cultural impact of coeducation.

Great good accrued from the advent of coeducation at the Commonwealth's public college in the 1920s and 1930s. Women reaped the rewards of higher learning, and the institution benefited from their talents and contributions.

Something else happened, too. Men and women mingled on campus. Sometimes they fell in love and went on to marry, making memories of youthful days spent on the campus in Amherst a shared marital experience, a golden thread that wound its way through decades of family life.

When Ellsworth Barnard, class of '28, was a young post-graduate instructor at Massachusetts State College he met undergraduate Mary Taylor Barnard '34, and when dating escalated to marriage, they took a place among the first such couples. In 1977, they compared notes about their time on campus.

On botany professor Ray "Doc" Torrey

ELLSWORTH: Ray Torrey was by all odds the greatest teacher I ever had anywhere. He had a very magnetic personality, for one thing . . . "Doc" Torrey had a discussion group on Friday evenings at his home. These discussions were participated in by a group of about eight to ten students; usually good students and usually male, in my day. I was invited by a fraternity brother. From then on, every Friday night was reserved for going to Doc Torrey's. We discussed philosophical and religious questions. We started with a text. One year we spent almost the entire year on the Bhagavad Gita. Another time it was one of the Gospels.

State College couples dancing, 1944

MARY: Those evenings were very, very wonderful. I never had a feeling that he looked down on the girls in any way. In my first year of going to the group I was so awed and impressed by the people. . . . I had the feeling in my senior year that Doc might have liked to have some of us go into theosophy, but up until that time I had never had any feeling that he was trying to push us in any way. He was just trying to pull things out of us, interest us in expanding our minds. . . . His lectures were just electric. He drew in philosophy and history and religion and music and literature—into botany lectures!

ELLSWORTH: In his first lecture in freshman botany he would do that particularly, and the kids would come out with their heads whirling.

On English professor Frank Prentice Rand:

ELLSWORTH: [Professor Rand] had what I thought was . . . a good system in one creative writing course I took with him: He would have us each choose a general area, and he would make theme assignments for each of us on topics within that area. My topic was "a farm boy and nature." I remember some of the topics—a farm boy meets the birds, moon magic, preseasonal frost. Some of my best papers came out of that class.

On the broad range of required classes:

MARY: I think those requirements were, in the long run, an advantage. Because you had a chance to sample. I find it very hard to understand how kids are going to know whether they want something or not if they've never been introduced to it at all. Some of the young people we see now just don't want to try anything new. That's too bad, really, because they're possibly missing an opportunity to find something they'd be really excited about.

The Barnards may have been among the first couples to meet at the state college and go on to start a family, but they were far from the last. In the twenty-first century, the university counts some eight *thousand* married couples among its alumni. It's a group with an extraordinarily strong bond to their alma mater. In 2005, UMass sent an impressively successful fundraising appeal to these couples, a pink envelope containing a Valentine's Day greeting:

> One dozen red roses: $74.99. . . .
> Being a UMass Amherst alumni couple: Priceless.

After decades of relatively modest expansion and change, the state college was about to blow out all the stops, its student body multiplying sixfold between 1945 and 1960, its grounds—amounting to some seven hundred acres now—sprouting well over a hundred new buildings in roughly the same period. It was an unruly, extraordinarily energetic process, driven by a sentiment that was animating change all over the country: the determination that Americans *would* have their long-awaited peace and prosperity and that the G.I.s streaming home from far-flung theaters of war would be the first to benefit.

Provisions of the so-called G.I. Bill, passed in 1943 and 1944, gave these service men and women the right to a college education at government expense. Veterans proved more than eager to take up this opportunity. By May 1946 Massachusetts was reporting that some 2,800 eligible vets had been turned away from colleges in the state for simple lack of capacity. The state college was in no way ready to receive this flood of eager students, but as a public institution it bore the greatest responsibility for doing its utmost.

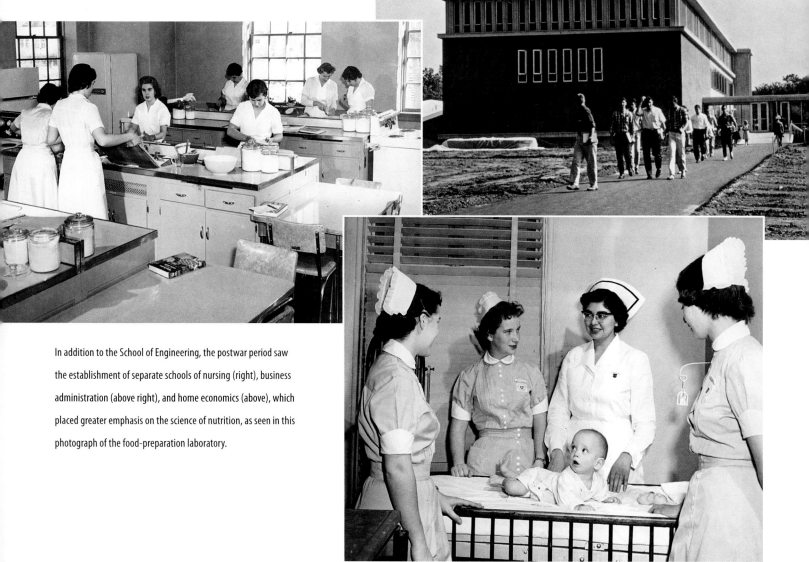

In addition to the School of Engineering, the postwar period saw the establishment of separate schools of nursing (right), business administration (above right), and home economics (above), which placed greater emphasis on the science of nutrition, as seen in this photograph of the food-preparation laboratory.

In December 1941, shortly after the country entered World War II, Paul O. Dickinson Jr., a student at Massachusetts State College, enlisted in the U.S. Coast Guard, making him among the first of the school's many students who would do so. Some three and half years later, with the war coming to a close, now-Executive Officer Dickinson wrote to Dean William Machmer "to apologize for leaving school without saying thank you for what you did for me." Dean Machmer's reply gave the young man a sharp-focused picture of what awaited him should he decide to re-enroll at the college.

July 9, 1945

My dear Mr. Dickinson:

Your letter of June 24th is very much appreciated. How well I remember the day you were admitted as well as the one on which you withdrew in order to join the Coast Guard. Nineteen forty-one and forty-two were exciting years here on the campus. Those men students who continued their courses did so under mixed emotions. There was the urge to enlist. Ultimately we lost practically all our men.

Fortunately, however, we are a co-educational Institution and the number of girls has steadily increased until we now have a few over six hundred in our regular degree course. We cannot go beyond this until additional facilities are provided. Even under the present arrangement, it is necessary for us to house the women students in North College, the men's fraternity houses. This coming year we are going to use Lewis and Thatcher Halls for women.

Now that the War with Germany is ended, we are beginning to get some of the old students discharged from the service. At the present moment there are seventeen of these enrolled in the college. This number will be thirty or forty at least when the fall semester opens.

It is my sincere hope that when the War is over, you too may find it possible to continue your course with us. We will be glad to welcome you back. You will find that during your absence the college has made a very substantial contribution toward the War effort—not only has it trained thousands of the pre-flight Army Trainees, but it has also given, besides its entire student body of men, a great many of the fine young members of the faculty. It has also offered all types of short courses to help in fitting men for necessary work in vital war industries. We shall hope to write up these accomplishments rather fully and I am sure that it will make a record of which we may all feel proud.

President Hugh P. Baker and Dean William Machmer, World War II–era administrators

In spite of the varied and thrilling experiences which you have had, you apparently came through them all sound in mind and body. It is my hope that you will continue to be equally fortunate while winding up the Japanese campaign.

With all good wishes.

Sincerely yours,

Dean Machmer

It faced a critical dearth of facilities. During the Depression and war years, with help from the federal Emergency Public Works Administration, alumni donations, and an alumni building association bond issue, the campus had gained a library (Goodell) and gym (Curry Hicks) as well as dorms Thatcher, Lewis, and Butterfield. But this had been barely sufficient to accommodate the pre-war student body of 1,700 or so—much less than the thousands vying for a spot in 1946.

At the close of World War II, when huge numbers of veterans and wartime industrial workers came knocking at the doors of higher education, Massachusetts found itself completely unprepared to receive them.

The Commonwealth had a very long tradition of relying on private colleges to educate its citizens (indeed these powerful institutions did not necessarily favor the expansion of more affordable rivals). Among the states, Massachusetts ranked near the bottom in opportunities for low-cost, public higher education.

Explosive post-war growth at the college would improve these opportunities, but in the meantime, the demand constituted a practical and even an ethical emergency. Massachusetts veterans *deserved* to benefit from the G.I. Bill.

Responding to the urgency of the moment, at the behest of the governor, educators of the state—including the presidents of Massachusetts State College (soon to become UMass), Harvard, Massachusetts Institute of Technology, Boston University, Tufts, and other colleges—formed a committee to found and oversee a temporary campus at a former military installation, Fort Devens in eastern Massachusetts, which would be a satellite of M.S.C.

They started planning in the spring of 1946. In July administrators sent letters to eligible vets. Brick barracks would be dorms. Former warehouses, maintenance shops, theaters, and garages would be labs and classrooms. An old bakery would serve as a machine shop.

The administrators scoured the territory for faculty, who were in short supply and could be offered only a temporary assignment at no more than the usual, relatively low state scale. Nevertheless some 125 came on board, and, five days before school was to open in the autumn of 1946, they turned out in overalls to move clothes lockers, chairs, beds, and bedding into four three-story buildings to serve as dormitories. "It must be remembered," commented a 1949 report on the Devens campus by the American Council on Education, "that at this period the entire country was stirred by an intense emotional desire to do something real for the veterans."

More than 1,300 men showed up at Fort Devens that fall, and between 1946 and 1949, when the campus closed, a total of 2,686 attended. All had qualified academically; roughly half of the applications had been rejected on that basis. Their average age was 22.1 years; by 1948 one in five Devens students was married.

In just a few months, the state college along with leaders of other private colleges planned a satellite campus of Massachusetts State College at a military installation called Fort Devens in eastern Massachusetts. Administrators quickly hired instructors and retrofitted barracks for college life. "The physical plant at Devens reserved for our use includes some 250 buildings. (Each has its own heating plant—there are problems!)," said a memo from the president's office. "Every effort will be made to eliminate any suggestion of

Fort Devens students show their spirit.

The students received freshman and sophomore classes in sciences, the humanities, and social studies. More remarkable was the flowering of extracurricular activities on such short notice: a newspaper and magazine, glee club, orchestra, and band, as well as French Club and Automotive Club developed. Weekly "Devens Tuesdays" offered lectures, concerts, and discussions.

These were men who had grown up fast in a brutal age; they were eager for civilian life and culture in all their facets. Devens president Edward Hodnett wrote a note to one such young man, Morton Cohen, about a play that Cohen had written. "It is a notable first effort," Hodnett remarked. "Obviously, men would be better off without the experience that permits you to write and then to comprehend such a holocaust; but since the experience has become a major part of your view of the world, you have done well in distilling it. I hope that you will go on writing about the essentials as they strike you."

The Devens experiment was far from ideal. Students complained about the crowded, noisy barracks and mess-hall food—unwelcome reminders, perhaps, of military life. But some 60 percent left the campus to continue their college careers, in Amherst or elsewhere. Devens was their new beginning. "[It] offered a chance for a college education when all other ways were closed," one vet wrote later. "There was laid the groundwork for my further study."

military affairs and offer a sound and solid college program." The plan was for Devens to provide the first two years' training, with students eligible for transfer later to the main campus. Some 1,300 vets thronged the installation in the autumn of 1946.

Back in Amherst, appropriations came through for a new physics lab, animal pathology lab, and home economics building. Work began on two new dorms, Chadbourne and Greenough, but in July 1946 it was apparent that, due to labor shortages and slow delivery of steel and other supplies, the buildings wouldn't be ready for the autumn influx. A campus committee decided three hundred students would have to be accommodated by "setting up beds and other facilities in buildings providing large, dormitory-style rooms and adequate adjacent lavatory facilities." Temporary married-student housing, dubbed Federal Circle, went up in clusters on the west side of Lincoln Avenue; behind Draper Hall, rickety barracks-style buildings for some 240 single vets bore the anomalously grand name of Commonwealth Circle. Acting president Ralph Van Meter appealed to teaching

America emerged from World War II the world's preeminent economic and technological power. To maintain and build on that superiority, the federal government poured resources into science and engineering.

What did this mean for UMass students? Opportunity—especially for those with engineering degrees. Paths opened up that graduates in the far more constricted economic environment of the 2010s would surely envy.

Although the college had offered education in agricultural engineering for many years, it wasn't until just after the institution's designation as the University of Massachusetts in 1947 that the School of Engineering was born. It offered four major departments—in agricultural, electrical, mechanical, and civil engineering. Chemical engineering was introduced the next year. From 1949 through 1965, the UMass campus gained five engineering buildings at a cost of nearly $7 million. The school grew rapidly, graduating 250 in 1951.

During the 1950s, growing companies competed for trained manpower, pitching themselves in the UMass *Collegian* as hospitable, exciting places to work. From the defense technology company Raytheon: "Join a progressive dynamic company that is setting new records in the electronic industry. Seniors and graduate students: Openings for: electrical engineers, chemical engineers, mechanical engineers, physicists." Another ad touted the "creative engineering by Western Electric men." "Engineers of all skills—mechanical, electrical, chemical, industrial, metallurgical, and civil—are needed to help us show the way in fundamental manufacturing techniques," it said.

The giant General Electric (GE) launched an apprenticeship program with UMass whose benefits, in today's context, seem quite extraordinary.

"Suppose your son is accepted as an engineering apprentice at GE's great transformer plant in Pittsfield, Mass.," ran a 1957 piece in *Popular Science*. "He will go onto

staff to help the registrar and dean's office process an avalanche of paperwork. "It cannot be handled without assistance," wrote Van Meter, who would formally replace Baker as president in 1948 and serve through the mid-1950s. "Any time that you can give will be appreciated."

The old debate about university status had been completely overtaken by events; it was clear the Commonwealth needed such an institution, sooner rather than later. On May 6, 1947, the governor signed legislation remaking the state college into the University of Massachusetts. Right away the institution began to send out fresh shoots. New courses approved for 1947—ranging from water-color painting to paleontology to principles of journalism to advanced quantitative analysis—give an idea of the increasing specialization and diversity. Devens closed in 1949, with 40 percent of students transferring to the Amherst campus, where great quantities of earth were being upturned as construction continued apace.

the payroll right away, full-time. Also right away, he and about 30 other young men will start a training program that will last four years. He will rotate work assignments in the machine shop, drafting room and engineering office. In addition, for nine hours each week—evenings and Saturday mornings—he will attend classes taught by instructors from the University of Massachusetts. . . . At the end of the four-year program he will be graduated as an engineering technician with two years of college credit." Sound like a good deal? The apprentice also received raises every six months and the option to continue for a four-year UMass degree at company expense. *Popular Science* enthused, "The company may even give him time off with pay—as much as four hours a week—to study."

Engineering in the 1950s

School of Engineering grads in the 1950s went to work for an array of corporations taking part in the post-war industrial boom—from Eastman Kodak to Westinghouse to Singer Manufacturing to Sylvania Electric Products to Monsanto Chemical Company.

In 1955, an executive of the New York Air and Brake Company came to campus to give a rousing talk on the promise of this period. The country's "stupendous emphasis on research expenditure," he said, "has evolved a revolution of man against things as they are when there are ways of doing things better. It is an intelligent struggle against ignorance and helplessness when there is so much that needs to be done to enable men and women to lead richer, fuller, and more satisfying lives."

Soon after the birth of the state university, its College of Agriculture was born; this administrative unit would house all of the school's work in horticulture and agriculture, including the extension service and the two-year program known as the Stockbridge School of Agriculture. After the wartime ramping up of the military-industrial complex, the country anticipated a peacetime boom in technological development—and a great need for trained engineers. Not to be left behind, UMass founded its School of Engineering in 1947, recruiting faculty from around the country. High-achieving students flocked to engineering; by the late 1950s, that school alone included nearly one thousand students. Nine faculty began teaching business courses in what, in 1947, was officially designated the School of Business Administration; a few years later this school boasted some 550 students, 60 percent more than were enrolled in the College of Agriculture.

Just as urgently as it needed engineers, the burgeoning country needed nurses and teachers. The university's School of Nursing was founded in 1953. Its teacher-training program, begun in 1907 with courses for instructors in agriculture, blossomed into a full-scale School of Education in 1956, one year after the liberal arts and sciences were joined to become the College of Arts and Sciences.

CRITICAL MASS

During the 1950s, the campus was fairly bursting with the pent-up energy of all the stinting years that came before. As UMass gained in size and quality, it began to take on something else—stature. The so-called Freedom Bill of 1956 sprung the university from state strictures to the extent that it could select talented faculty members and offer them salary incentives. Notables from Robert Frost to Eleanor Roosevelt came to address UMass audiences. During this period UMass increasingly cooperated with nearby Amherst, Mount Holyoke, and Smith Colleges in pooling resources to offer joint courses and academic appointments in subjects that lay off the beaten path. In 1959 a group of professors from these educational institutions launched the *Massachusetts Review*, which right away attracted the country's leading thinkers as both contributors and readers. From the outset, this journal was set up as a showcase for writers of nontraditional and under-represented literary arenas. Major sporting events—now embellished with a marching band and a cheerleading squad—drew large crowds and were sometimes even televised.

Women students faced something of a setback with the return of war veterans, who had official priority for admission. They were, for example, largely excluded from the prestigious School of Engineering. In 1952, the administration set a policy of maintaining 40 percent female students at the university, a goal that was not reached until much later. But UMass women of the period tended to be high achievers (their grade-point averages topping men's), and in Dean of Women Helen Curtis, who came in 1947 and served through 1973, they had both a friend and a savvy, determined advocate.

UMass students enjoyed the 1950s college scene in all its boisterous and sometimes downright goofy glory. There were sock hops and carnival queens. Chief Metawampe, a local Native American during early colonial days, became the university's official mascot in

1948, its sports teams dubbed Redmen. A women's living quad developed in what would later be known as the Northeast Residential Area, a men's quad in the latter-day Central Residential Area. A section of Eastman Lane was known as Lovers' Lane. The punctilious reining-in of freshmen gave way to an uproarious communalism. Of one September evening festivity, the *Collegian* noted, "a howling mob of freshmen stormed into the [Curry Hicks] Cage Saturday night for the first frosh inter-dorm sing, and at the same time yelled their way into complete acceptance as members of the University." If the stone chapel had symbolized the college's emergence from an uncertain beginning in the nineteenth century, perhaps no new building better expressed the post-war campus culture than the Student Union, completed in 1957, where students mingled, bowled and played table and board games, studied, dined, and ran various clubs and activities.

Meanwhile, Federal Circle, the temporary housing for married students, soon drew the moniker Maternity Row. Laundry flapped on clotheslines and children played in the communal yard. Here was the Baby Boom. Here was the college's future—and UMass leaders saw it coming. In the mid-1950s, Provost Jean Paul Mather, soon to become president, told an opening convocation that the rising generation of would-be collegians was three times the size of the current one and had as much right to an education as the four thousand students then enrolled. It wouldn't fall to institutions like Amherst, Tufts, and Williams to accommodate this massive wave of young people, he said. "These fine small colleges have announced their intention to set limits of unit size, skim the intellectual cream, and stand by. . . . [But] the horizon of our responsibility is that we cannot turn them away here."

Preparing for centennial celebrations of 100 years of public higher education in Massachusetts

In 1960, as the onetime "cow college" rounded its first century, a new leader, John Lederle, arrived from the University of Michigan to take the presidency. A man of large aspirations, Lederle would prove well fitted to the job ahead. "I have come to feel that what we have here is potentially a giant," he said early in his tenure. "I do not mean merely a bricks and mortar giant, but a great public center for excellence in higher education in the region."

An important function of a yearbook is to capture a sense of its times, just as *The Index* did in its editions for 1951 (above) and 1959 (opposite).

Homecoming 1955. In the chill October night, an excited crowd gathers near Memorial Hall. Now the parade is on the move; the Redmen marching band leads, followed by the drill team, the cheerleaders, and the drum majorettes. Up Lincoln Avenue, down Amity Street, past the movie theater, around the common, and back to the football field for that great communal expression of spirit, the Homecoming rally. "Lengthy and high-schoolish yells are taboo," says the *Collegian*. "Whereas peppy and rhythmic cheers are the order of the day." Finally, a mammoth bonfire, then bopping and swinging till the wee hours at Memorial Hall.

You just had to love college life in the 1950s. The country had been through a terrible wringer but emerged full of pride and optimism. Middle-class youth thronged the dorms and lecture halls in unprecedented numbers. The painful political and generational conflicts of the 1960s and 1970s lay in wait in a still-unimagined future. It was, at least for those with an amenable temperament, *fun.*

At UMass, readers of the *Collegian* could pick up the "latest recordings" at the Jeffery Amherst Music Shop. The new college radio station, WMUA, broadcast live jazz sessions from Skinner Hall—"jazz 'concerts' in every sense of the word," according to the organizers, "not stiff, formalized programs. If you play in a combo or would like to sit in on one of these groups, call Bob Hartwell at WMUA."

The Cold War was intensifying, with plenty of talk about the "Reds"—one student, a former *Collegian* editor, even testified before the Subversive Activities Control Board about possible Communist sympathies on campus. But mostly the military presence at UMass had an air of pomp and polish as well as the usual discipline. The annual Military Ball was a particularly lavish affair with full orchestra—"soft, danceable music," according to a press announcement, led by a trumpeter who "blows clear enough for all to hear but people can still carry on a conversation." The day of the dance, the college paper would run a headline along the lines of "Which One of These Lovely Ladies Will Be Honorary Colonel Tonight?" along with headshots of the perfectly coiffed, smiling "co-eds" who had been nominated. In fact there was a queen for every season—a Homecoming Queen, a Winter Carnival Snow Queen, and a Greek Ball Queen in the spring.

It was an unprecedented age in America. But on the deepest level, what animated the post-war builders of UMass was the same spirit that drove its founders. "We are pledged," said Lederle, "to the right of every individual, regardless of race, religion, or economic background, to that amount and kind of education of which he is capable, and for which he has the desire and will."

As for men, campus newspaper pages abounded with ads for Wildroot Cream-oil to tame fluffy hair and cowlicks—the bane of would-be suitors. Getting a varsity letter was a major coup; spoofing and cavorting (and sometimes dressing as women with large prosthetic breasts) were traditional in the annual school Variety Show. Nearly half the student body had pledged to a fraternity or sorority.

The College Store or "C Store," for a long time located in North College but moved to the Student Union upon its completion in 1957, was a popular hangout. It sold all sorts of supplies in addition to food, such as burgers and malteds. The biggest seller? Cigarettes. In the mid-1950s, the C Store sold 120 to 160 cartons a week.

But this particular form of college life, with all its own energy and style, wouldn't last long. The new generation then fledging would bring dramatic change to UMass—indeed, to campuses all across the country.

1964 Phi Beta Kappa chapter established

- Southwest Residential Complex constructed

1965 Commuter campus opens in Boston

- McGuirk Alumni Stadium completed

1966 Morrill Science Center completed

- Lederle Graduate Research Center built

- Whitmore Administration Building built

- Curfews for women abolished

1967 Undergraduate tuition for Massachusetts citizens = $200

1968 Committee for Collegiate Education of Black Students helps enroll 128 students

- Campus performances by Stan Getz, Simon and Garfunkel, Stevie Wonder; speeches by Johnny Carson, Dick Gregory, and Arthur Schlesinger

1969 First co-ed dorm, Greenough, approved

- Herter Hall erected

- Campus transit system begins

1970 UMass system established with five coequal campuses

- Oswald Tippo succeeds Lederle, becoming first chancellor of University of Massachusetts

- Enrollment = 23,389; graduate students = 4,500

UMASS

THE UNIVERSITY OF MASS

- Afro-American Studies Department founded

- Murray D. Lincoln Campus Center built

- Student strike protests invasion of Cambodia

1971 Randolph Bromery becomes chancellor

- Julius Erving ("Dr. J"), having led UMass to its first two conference championships, wraps up UMass career

1972 Everywoman's Center opened

- "Redmen" abandoned in favor of "Minutemen"

1973 Total enrollment = 24,138

- Library tower completed; later named for W. E. B. Du Bois

1974 Fine Arts Center built

1975 State fiscal crisis leads to protests against budget cuts; hiring freeze put in place

- Total enrollment = 25,884

- Pioneer Valley Transit Authority established

1976 In-state tuition = $345

1977 Faculty union, the Massachusetts Society of Professors, established

1979 Henry Koffler succeeds Bromery as chancellor

- Total enrollment = 24,012; more than 3,000 from outside the Commonwealth

1982 Joseph Duffey replaces Koffler as chancellor

1985 Stonewall Center created

RISING

HUSETTS AMHERST AT 150

I do not mean merely a bricks and mortar giant, but a great public center
for excellence in higher education in the region."

—*Chancellor John Lederle, 1961*

UMASS COMES OF AGE

The Growth Years

RETURNING VETERANS AND NEWLY EMANCIPATED YOUNG WOMEN OF THE WORLD WAR II GENERATION CREATED AN ALL-HANDS-ON-DECK EMERGENCY AT THE COMMONWEALTH'S STATE COLLEGE, REQUIRING QUICK, CREATIVE STRATEGIES FOR EXPANSION.

But the expansion that made the college into a bona fide university in 1947 was nothing compared with changes that would come when the war generation launched its great passel of offspring into a booming post-war economy. Coming of age, these children—the Baby Boomers—burst the seams of the University of Massachusetts, dramatically increasing its size. They also created a questioning, outspoken youth culture that swept the country and deeply marked the university's identity.

UMass's growth during the 1960s—in terms of enrollment, facilities, and budget—was unprecedented in its century of history and has not been repeated in the half-century that followed. A golden age of sorts, this growth period also represented a gargantuan undertaking.

A GROWING MIDDLE CLASS CHOOSES COLLEGE

The Baby Boom's demographic bulge took place during a time when Americans, in sharp contrast to the skeptical Massachusetts farmers of M.A.C.'s early days, were sold on higher education as the way to a prosperous, civilized way of life. As one parent wrote to UMass president John Lederle during a rather typical episode of late-1960s campus unrest, "I realize you have quite a serious problem to solve. Never having attended college, but always having the desire to and hoping my children could, I say a prayer for you and wish you the very best of luck."

While the state's august private colleges limited their growth and increasingly drew high-achieving students from around the country, UMass strained to accommodate surging state-wide demand for an affordable college education. Annual applications for a spot in the freshman class spiked, from just over 5,000 in 1959 to more than 20,000 a decade later. Though many had to be turned away, enrollment grew precipitously, nearly tripling in the decade leading up to 1972; during that same 10 years, the ratio of college-age Massachusetts citizens attending UMass itself climbed from one in 150 to one in 45. Even so, given the admissions squeeze, the SAT scores of entering classes steadily rose during this "Dynamic Decade."

A map from 1968 shows a campus radically transformed, with the Lederle Graduate Research Center, the Campus Center, Herter Hall, and parts of Southwest all in planning or under construction.

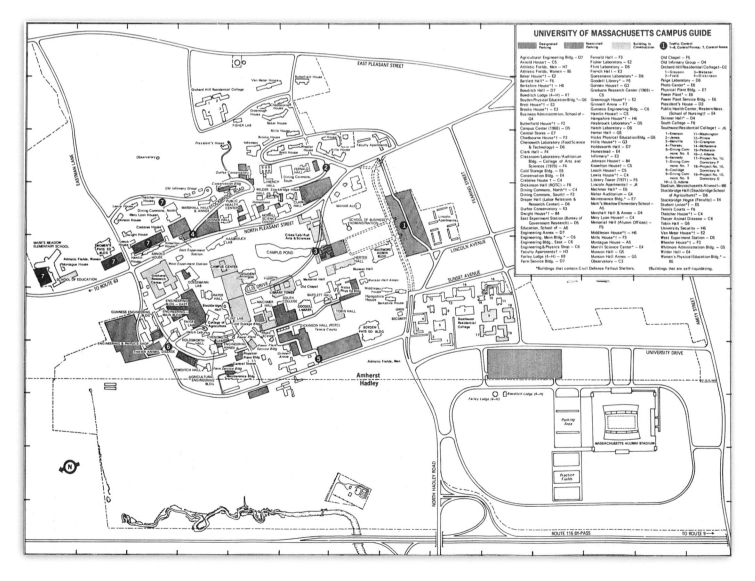

Class of 1968 (Freshman Convocation)

The university crammed its physical plant to the rafters, admitting "swing-shift freshmen"—those slightly less qualified—to attend in the summer, then return in the spring semester, when enrollment naturally declined through graduations and attrition. These hordes of young people picked their way across a campus pitted with freshly dug foundations. UMass owned about 1.4 million square feet of building space in 1950, rising to 2.9 million square feet in 1960. By 1970 the once bucolic cow college was covered by 7.2 million square feet of building space.

Every year the university brought on new faculty and other employees, with the full-time instructional staff growing by double digits most years of the 1960s; by 1972, faculty were one thousand strong.

A HIGH NEW ROAD

Despite the Commonwealth's traditional neglect of public higher education—a history stemming partly from its wealth of private institutions that, not coincidentally, clustered near the seat of political power in the east—UMass leadership of the 1960s had every intention of creating an institution that was not just big, but top-tier. This period saw the growth of its highly regarded engineering program, as well as the introduction of stellar research and graduate programs in, for example, computer science (a

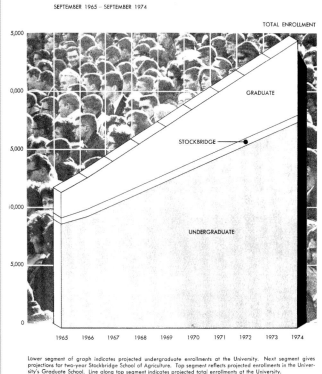

Long Range Enrollment Projection

SEPTEMBER 1965 – SEPTEMBER 1974

TOTAL ENROLLMENT

GRADUATE

STOCKBRIDGE

UNDERGRADUATE

1965 1966 1967 1968 1969 1970 1971 1972 1973 1974

Lower segment of graph indicates projected undergraduate enrollments at the University. Next segment gives projections for two-year Stockbridge School of Agriculture. Top segment reflects projected enrollments in the University's Graduate School. Line along top segment indicates projected total enrollments at the University.

These projections are for the campus in Amherst only; they do not include projected enrollments at the University of Massachusetts-Boston or the University's Medical School.

The ten-year enrollment projections from 1965 proved to be quite accurate, with enrollment reaching 25,884 by 1975.

There's a wonderful moment in the 1967 movie *The Graduate* in which a suburban neighbor leans in to Dustin Hoffman's young character and says, "I just want to say one word to you. Just one word. Are you listening? *Plastics.*"

While the line's intent is satirical, it also spoke a truth. The plastics field was indeed in the midst of an energetic flowering in the 1960s. Mammoth American chemical and manufacturing companies—GE, Dow, Monsanto, 3M—were working at top capacity to produce materials that were lighter, more flexible, stronger, and more heat resistant. With Cold War fears mounting, the government was ready to pour funds into work that promised to yield similar results.

The trouble was, few people understood the basic properties of polymers, the special molecules that make up these materials. Industrial labs had to hire graduates in chemistry, physics, or engineering, then train them in polymer science, which brings together all three disciplines. Founders of the UMass polymer science program perceived this breach and were determined to fill it.

The work began in 1961 under Richard Stein, who was soon joined by William MacKnight and others. From the beginning, recalls MacKnight, the idea was to establish an emphatically interdisciplinary program, pulling together expertise from across UMass's science and engineering departments. The Polymer Science and Engineering Program awarded its first degrees in 1968, and they were bestowed only upon graduate students who had attained this advanced and specialized state of knowledge.

Three members of the faculty who were instrumental in launching the UMass polymer science program: (from left) Roger Porter, the first director, Robert Lenz, and William MacKnight, 1969.

In 1973 the program pulled off a major coup, convincing the federal government to establish at UMass the first materials research lab devoted strictly to polymeric materials. "Because of the speed and dimensions of plastics growth," the university's proposal for the Materials Research Laboratory observed, "it is important to examine the national posture in polymer research. This is the foundation upon which future technological advances will be based, and our national economic position in materials demands that the research and development situation cannot be left to chance."

In 1980 another breakthrough came with the establishment of the Center for UMass/ Industry Research on Polymers (CUMIRP), which included support from some 20 industrial partners. According to MacKnight, the benefit for these companies in the early days was not exclusively—even primarily—the center's research yields so much as giving them "a crack at our students." Like professional sports recruiters, "they could follow the students right from day one and get a pretty good handle on which ones would best suit their needs."

Formally opened in 1996, the multimillion-dollar Silvio O. Conte National Center for Polymer Research sealed UMass's reputation in the field. This state-of-the-art facility helped the university attract the best and brightest by offering access to the "dream machines" required for advanced research, as MacKnight calls them.

Inquiry at UMass into the complex behavior of polymers contributed basic insights that ultimately helped produce an array of everyday products. Faculty worked on finding ways to combine materials that take advantage of their different properties—mixing, for example, a cheap product with an expensive one that can be used at high temperatures. They helped figure out how to make a less-brittle glasslike material, which led to development of headlights that resist damage from flung pebbles. They addressed the problem of how to make curled and tangled threadlike molecules "line up in an elongated way, like a pile of logs," as MacKnight puts it, which produces the enormous strength of materials used in bulletproof vests.

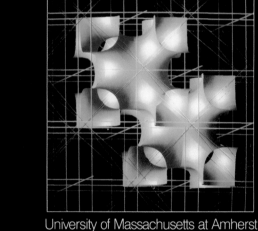
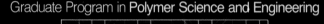

Graduate Program in **Polymer Science and Engineering**

University of Massachusetts at Amherst

Perhaps even more importantly, over the years UMass has seeded industry and academia across the country and the world with trained specialists in polymer science. One instance is alumna Cady Coleman, who received her Ph.D. in polymer science and engineering in 1991. The following year she was selected to join the NASA Astronaut Corps, and she made her first space flight as a Mission Specialist aboard the space shuttle *Columbia* in 1995. In 2011, Coleman delivered the UMass Amherst Commencement address—from space—because she was in the midst of a six-month stint aboard the International Space Station at the time.

Vice President George P. Burns explains the features of a computerized milling machine to Professor Geoffry Boothroyd and engineering students Peter Rogers and Laurence Murch.

prescient investment obviously) and polymer science (a research niche that anticipated the explosion in the role of plastics and other synthetic materials in modern industry). Indeed, the graduate school generally burgeoned, with a headcount of some 750 students in 1960 growing to 4,500 in 1970.

UMass was gamely upping the ante, increasing its scholarly profile and output. By the early 1960s, the *Massachusetts Review* was, according to a yearbook, "being read in Boston and San Francisco, in Ottawa and in New Orleans, in Houston and Honolulu, in Tokyo, Amsterdam, Munich, Vienna and Rome." The University of Massachusetts Press began publishing titles in 1963 to respectful reviews. Around the same time the university purchased a nuclear reactor, so physics students could study the half-lives of radioactive materials, and an early computing system, the Control Data 3600, mostly for graduate and faculty research.

By the late 1960s, the charming old Goodell Library bulged with more than a million volumes. The college consortium of UMass Amherst with Amherst, Mount Holyoke, and Smith Colleges had established an active exchange among the campuses. In 1970, when Hampshire College joined, the group adopted the Five College Consortium as its official name. That students at any one of these local colleges could draw on the others' resources—borrow books, take courses, attend events—was a selling point for all. In 1964 UMass met the stringent academic standards required to launch a chapter of Phi Beta Kappa, something the dean of the business school called a "great leap forward." In 1967 UMass took over the license for the consortium's public radio station, WFCR, which began broadcasting from Hampshire House. A fledgling transit service using old school buses carried students around the growing UMass plant.

UMass was, by the close of the turbulent 1960s, a stimulating community of tens of thousands of people—a magnet that drew interesting figures looking to instruct, entertain, or persuade. In 1968, the campus enjoyed performances by Stan Getz, Stevie Wonder, and Simon and Garfunkel. Numerous speakers came to discuss their ideas on timely issues: Dick Gregory spoke about racism and Black Power and Arthur Schlesinger, a former assistant to presidents Kennedy and Johnson, discussed the war in Vietnam. Johnny Carson declined to discuss Vietnam, but he did argue against the legalization of marijuana, which he deemed "psychologically addicting."

All this growth would not have been possible without a truly massive influx of funds. In the decade between 1962 and 1972, the UMass budget ballooned 700 percent. President Lederle was an effective lobbyist, working with a state legislature whose stance toward the public university was more than ordinarily beneficent during this period. He also raised money from the federal government.

Indeed Lederle's leadership was critical; he was a man of vaulting ambition, driven by some of the same populist ideals voiced by the land-grant college's nineteenth-century founders. "We are now embarked on the most dynamic program of educational renewal and improvement in the whole history of the Commonwealth and perhaps of the country itself," he wrote. Lederle believed UMass could "shape the enlightened citizen of tomorrow" and "further the aims of a free society." The university at Amherst would be "a high new road . . . to be traveled by all those who seek knowledge and its benefits."

A DIFFERENT VIEW

However determined UMass leaders were to shape a generation, it was the youth themselves who really set the agenda; they swamped the campus, their sheer numbers shifting its dynamics. "If teachers and administrators continue to retreat before every onslaught by students, the entire educational system in this country will be jeopardized," one indignant citizen wrote Lederle in the 1960s. "Students come to college to be educated, not to educate their teachers." But as the years wore on, it became clear these students had a distinctly different view of things.

The candidates for queen of the Military Ball, 1961

UMass yearbooks of the early 1960s betray some of the same cheerful ("stylized," as one administrator put it) accommodation of authority that characterized students of the 1950s. The Twist was still the craze, poet Robert Frost remained a household name and exemplar of cultural excellence, and the inexorably mounting

In the autumn of 1975, a Vietnam vet named Al Byam arrived at Amherst to begin his college education. He was a few years older than most of his classmates and, like a lot of vets, experienced beyond his years. It was quite a transition to make.

But before long Byam found a group of simpatico fellow students, many of them veterans as well, who worked as bus drivers and dispatchers for the fledgling UMass transit system. The transit hub, he says, "was a nice place to be, because the other veterans' organizations on campus were a little more radical at the time. This was a great group just trying to get on with their lives, get on with their school lives."

Charmed by the breed-apart, laid-back spirit of his fellow transit workers, Byam also found himself attracted to the work itself. "Working in operations is exciting," he says. "It's different every day. You have a snow day, maybe, or there's an accident. There's always something going on." Even so he couldn't have known that his first stint as a driver would

lead to a series of promotions ending in the top job at UMass Transit—a nearly four-decade career devoted to getting students and employees to class, to work, and to and from various off-campus communities safely and on time.

The transit system was still growing when Byam signed on. It had begun in 1969 as a simple campus circulator running old school buses and transit coaches along two daytime routes, one the so-called Super Loop around campus, the other linking the campus to an apartment complex in North Amherst and parking lots along University Drive.

In 1972, a UMass engineering professor and a grad student won a federal demonstration grant to offer a more substantial no-fare transit system, adding four new off-campus routes, 10 buses, and a small garage. Two years later the state created the Pioneer Valley Transit Authority (PVTA), which contracted with the existing UMass transit system to operate an expanded service; this brought 25 new buses and a new garage with office space and mechanics' bays. By 1975 the system had 145 part-time employees, ran weekends and late nights, and carried some 16,000 passengers daily. In 1982 it grew again, taking over from the Five Colleges some routes for transporting students to other nearby member campuses. Originally sponsored by the student senate, by now the system was funded through a combination of state, federal, and university sources.

By fits and starts, UMass Transit had become central to the life of UMass and, indeed, a model for the country.

tensions of the Cold War continued to be accepted without a great deal of fuss. One caption in the 1963 yearbook, below a picture of a couple at the annual Military Ball, teased, "Oh you big handsome cadet you—are you really going to protect me from those nasty Russians?"

"Fourteen years after it began hauling students, professors, and townspeople over the rural New England countryside in a zany collection of cast-off school buses," the *Lewiston Journal* remarked in 1983, "the University of Massachusetts bus system has graduated into one of the nation's largest and most successful no-fare transit systems."

The role of students in running the system is perhaps its most extraordinary feature. Entirely student operated until 1976, it remains mostly so in the twenty-first century. That means college students get trained (and paid) to drive commercial buses, among other jobs. "We have high standards here," a Transit Services assistant manager told the 1990 *Index*. "We set up the students' driving schedules initially, but then the students take care of it. Working for the UMass Transit is a 'real world' type job." Twenty years later, student computer science majors were creating maintenance records and schedules, driver schedules, and network management tools. "They're the brains behind the scenes for all kinds of things," observed operations manager Glenn Barrington.

Student bus driver Megan Voorhis

But the system's main benefits extend beyond the bus garage to the broader community. UMass Transit has been an antidote to the transportation disaster that might have developed in the area with the mid-twentieth-century decline of electric commuter railways, the rise of the automobile, and the massive growth of the campus itself.

An early motivation for the system was to provide students with an alternative to rampant hitchhiking. "Rumor has it that Volkswagens . . . have the most consideration for the wheelless," said a 1970s *Index*. But the extensive network of bus routes has prevented the "wheelless" from being isolated on campus. And it's forestalled the polluting—and maddening—gridlock that would ensue if every commuter drove a car. Meanwhile, UMass Transit has sought to make its own fleet as green as possible by adding hybrid vehicles to the fleet and using the cleanest-burning fuels available. In 2010, an independent evaluator gave UMass an A for environmental sustainability in transportation.

Keeping the service free hasn't been easy given the vagaries of the funding process, says Byam, who retired in 2013. But the fact that riders can hop on a bus to just about any place they'd want to go, at just about any hour—and without a dollar in their pockets—is precisely what makes the system work, he says. "My basic philosophy is that if a student has a dollar and has a choice between buying pizza, a beverage, or a bus fare, we're going to lose 99 percent of the time. Let's let them ride without thinking about it," he says. "Keep them safe at night."

Students in Goodell Library, ca. 1962

Change came abruptly. Within just a few years students had traded in pencil skirts and tailored blazers for ragged blue jeans and fringe. They were "rapping" about racism, sexuality, and the bloody toll in Vietnam. The yearbooks took on a serious and even dark cast, expressing a growing preoccupation, in this newly technological age, with how to maintain individuality in the collective—how to resist becoming, as Lederle himself put it, "a 'machined' product."

With an alacrity that alarmed many of their elders, these students changed the rules.

For all the years of the school's history, for example, UMass women (and female college students generally) had been unquestioningly subject to special curfews and dorm rules. "It's done," announced the *Collegian* in May 1966. "Curfews and other archaic rules for women have been abolished. But in a larger sense, we have just begun to lead." "In the fall," marveled the *Boston Globe*, "women students will be free to come and go as they please." The *Globe* concurred with the *Collegian* in calling the change "pace-setting."

Indeed, just a few years later a novel "open house policy" in effect removed restrictions against students of the opposite sex socializing together at any hour they chose, not just in common areas but also in their dorm rooms. In a survey on the new policy, one student remarked, "For the first time in my three years here, the University has recognized the desperate need for privacy: privacy to study, to talk, to cry—even to kiss—without 16,000 people watching and/or listening."

Fast upon the heels of the "open" single-sex residence hall came co-ed dorms. Greenough was the first, the result of a student initiative approved by the trustees in the fall of

President Lederle with a group of students in the Student Union's Colonial Lounge

1969. In the spring of 1970, 44 women moved in, occupying separate floors from male residents. By the middle of that semester, 12 more student proposals to take their dorms co-ed lay before UMass leaders. One was from Butterfield. "At UMass, most of the male-female relationships are developed within the dating situation," it read. "For this reason cultural-based sex roles and commercial images of ourselves dominate the relationships." Sharing space—and daily life—would change that, these students thought. They insisted that even the segregated-floor arrangement at Greenough perpetuated a We/They gender divide that should end. In 1971, the trustees removed rules excluding freshmen from co-ed dorms and allowed mixed-sex floors. Although some critics seethed, the zeitgeist was headed swiftly in the other direction; soon co-ed dorms were the norm, and even co-ed bathrooms appeared.

Senator Hubert H. Humphrey on campus, 1964

GETTING TOGETHER FOR CHANGE

Students of the 1960s and 1970s were intent upon rearranging a lot more of the world than just their dormitories, and collective action became their tool. UMass students spoke out against what they saw as unfair treatment of particular faculty members; they protested underrepresentation of African-American news in the *Collegian;* they agitated for better lighting on campus and objected to fee increases and on-campus recruiting by certain corporations. Some thumbed their noses at the academic enterprise itself. In awarding honors, quipped the 1969 *Index,* the university had "officially certified the thinking" of certain students. That same year one graduate, voted a "distinguished senior" by the faculty, belittled his accomplishments. "President of the Student Senate is very little," he said, "when I consider that I have never participated in a good sit-in or disrupted even one speaker. . . . I could have done better."

Some protests amounted to brawls or shout-downs, as in February 1970 when former vice president Hubert H. Humphrey was driven from the podium by yelling, stomping, and marshmallow- and confetti-flinging activists—behavior roundly condemned by the

From the May 5, 1970, *Daily Collegian*:

> With emotion and dedication running high but concerted planning lacking, the UMass Strike Committee yesterday brought the idea of a nation-wide student strike dramatically to this campus with spray-paint posters, dormitory teach-ins, and a great deal of rapping. Scheduled for today are picket lines in front of academic buildings and discussions in those classes which meet on the first day of the strike.

All night, students had overflowed the Student Union ballroom to vote and cheer for plans to join the mass action of dissent sweeping the country's campuses during the spring of 1970.

On April 29 the first American incursions into Cambodia began as part of the Vietnam conflict. President Nixon announced the invasion April 30. On May 2 and 3, students from UMass Amherst and other colleges flocked to New Haven, Connecticut, to support the so-called New Haven 8, Black Panthers on trial for allegedly killing an informant. The next day, May 4, added fuel to the fire; the Ohio National Guard fired on unarmed students protesting the Cambodian campaign at Kent State University. Four died; nine were wounded.

College students around the country erupted in anguish and outrage, coalescing around the national "strike" first called by students at Princeton University. At UMass and elsewhere three basic demands were being made: cessation of U.S. expansion of the war in Southeast Asia; an end to political oppression and release of prisoners like the New Haven 8; and a halt to military recruiting and research on campus.

Though tensions ran high, UMass administrators responded with restraint. They allowed the occupation of the Student Union on the grounds that it was supported with student fees and appointed volunteer marshals from among students and faculty to keep the peace. Campus police agreed not to enter striking areas unless invited by these marshals. Chancellor Oswald Tippo expressed support for the strike, calling Nixon's move into Cambodia "sheer madness." Faculty members

Some striking students staged a "run on the banks" to demonstrate a possible method for bringing a halt to the Vietnam War.

administration and much of the student body as well. Other mass events were mere larks, like the nude "streaking" that, at one point in the early 1970s, became so routine that some streakers adopted gimmicks like riding unicycles or carrying lit torches. "It's better than painting clenched fists on the buildings," remarked former president Lederle, who had just returned to his professorship in political science.

formed their own committee in support of the cause. The Mental Health Services staff placed an ad in the *Collegian*: "We are shocked and sickened by the mentality of war and oppression of political dissenters and minority groups. . . . . While we plan to continue offering appointments to students at the Mental Health Service, we fully support the strike and its aims, and we pledge our active participation."

After converging in the thousands on the lawn by North Pleasant Street, on the evening of May 5th students agreed to continue the strike. They also agreed it should be nonobstructive, meaning classes could go on, and those who chose to attend could do so unmolested. Spring Day was canceled. The student senate voted 66 to 1 to "strongly urge . . . all members of the University community as a matter of individual conscience and moral duty to participate in the nationwide student strike to end the war."

There was a strikers' "run on the banks" in Amherst to withdraw money and stop war dollars flowing. A protest in Dickinson Hall aimed to obstruct ROTC activities' administrative work, because "without paperwork few triggers would be pulled."

A new grading policy was announced as of May 4 that allowed students to simply pass a course, take an incomplete, or be graded on a partial or full term's work. "No student may be held responsible for any work or exams due after May 4 against his wishes," it said. "I went to a couple of workshops [on May 11 and 12] and saw a few teachers to see what they were doing about regularly scheduled school work," one student wrote in her diary of the events. "All my teachers were very cooperative when I told them I was participating in the strike. I took letter grades in all my courses."

Anti-war activism in Amherst

Many classes were turned into workshops on topics such as "Why Non-Violence?" and "Physics Research and the War." Some students even traveled to local high schools to teach.

Notwithstanding their inability to end the war in Vietnam (or political oppression for that matter), in general UMass community members felt good about what they'd done that spring. Avoiding the violence and intergenerational rancor so common on other campuses, they had made a point—for the most part, with one voice.

CRUCIBLES OF AN ERA

At the center of student mass action, however, were the great moral issues of the age, which washed over the UMass campus along with a massive wave of young students.

One of them was racial integration and the Civil Rights movement. By the mid-1960s, with well over 10,000 students at UMass, there were perhaps three dozen African-American students—more black students attended from Africa itself—and just a handful of black faculty members. These faculty, including soon-to-be UMass chancellor Randolph Bromery and the noted sociologist William Julius Wilson, joined forces to change that. Armed with a grant from the Ford Foundation, they went to urban areas in Springfield and Boston to find and woo minority students. By the fall of 1968 the Committee for the Collegiate Education of Black Students (CCEBS) had enrolled, with plans to support and retain, 128 black students—the institution's first African-American community.

During the 1970 student strike, this fist poster on the campus statue of Metawampe bore the description: "the legendary spirit of the Redmen."

Quite a lot, judging from the seemingly perennial debates about what to call UMass athletes. It has been no easy task to settle on a name—or mascot—that is at once an appropriate representation of institutional identity and powerful enough to inspire loyal supporters and whip up crowds. Among the suggestions floated over the years: Great Danes, bloodhounds, zebras, collies, bobcats, bulls, American Indians, avocados (really), pilgrims, and doves.

Originally, of course, you had the Aggies, a name inextricably tied to the agricultural focus of the school and the object of fierce debate for generations. The question arose again after World War II, when the college became the University of Massachusetts. The Statesmen, which came into play in 1931, when M.A.C. became Massachusetts State College, didn't seem right now that the institution was a university.

Students took a vote in 1947, with choices including Minutemen, Mohawks, Indians, Bulls, Pilgrims, Yankees, Pioneers, and Tomahawks. Results were split. Later that fall a student and a professor began promoting the name *Redmen,* and that November the student senate voted to place the question before students. They approved the change 620 to 459. The model for the mascot was local legend Chief Metawampe, who had lived in the Pioneer Valley in the mid-1600s. The class of 1950 gave the university its famous statue of the great chief.

This Indian name and mascot were intended to honor the native peoples of Massachusetts, their "courage, strength, resourcefulness, and charity" toward the first white settlers at Plymouth, as a 1967 internal memo noted. Still, sports teams often were referred to as "fighting Redmen"; and the aforementioned memo describes the Indians' determination to defend their homeland as "a strength and fierceness well suited to a football team defending its goal posts."

It was an uneasy community. The students—who came largely from underperforming schools—were culturally different, even from their black professors, and they were surrounded by white people who were curious about them and not uniformly friendly. The African-American students all lived in the Orchard Hill dorm complex, a policy that aimed to avoid isolating them from one another. Within a few months of their arrival on campus in the fall of 1968, a "racial incident" (as it was labeled in President Lederle's files) occurred that, while troubling, helped galvanize the establishment of black cultural and academic programs. The incident: A handful of white students set upon a black youth visiting from a nearby community college and his white host. The response: Black UMass students, calling themselves the Afro-American Organization, presented a list of 21 demands to the administration. They included a public apology from UMass leaders, punishment for racial harassment, money for black student activities, a black studies department, and

William Julius Wilson, sociology professor

Such trivializing comparisons, along with images of a cartoonish "Redman" in headdress and feathers dancing around at games and rallies, eventually met with disapprobation by Native Americans, not just at UMass but at many other colleges and universities with Native American mascots.

In 1972, a group of Native Americans from New York State wrote to the UMass administration objecting to the mascot's "undesirable racial connotations." Both the administration and student senate quickly agreed to change the name, mounting a student vote among three choices: Statesmen, Artichokes, and Minutemen. The minuteman—defender of Massachusetts during the American Revolution, deployed with lightning speed to face the British imperial threat wherever it might surface—won the day to become the new symbol.

At UMass, though, no lively conversation ever truly comes to an end. The Minuteman mascot became, in its turn, the center of controversy in the 1980s and again in the early 1990s when some students deemed the "white, gun-toting male" mascot too militaristic and exclusive of the women and nonwhite people who also played an important role in state history. But largely because of an outcry by alumni defending their alma mater's familiar mascot, the Minuteman with his trusty musket continues to stand his ground.

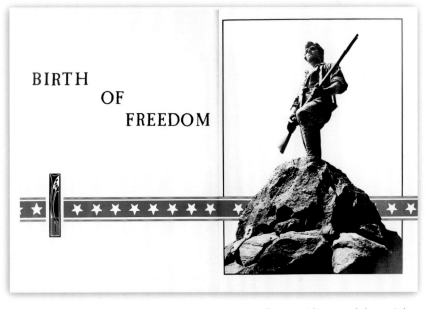

BIRTH OF FREEDOM

Anticipating the country's bicentennial, the 1975 *Index* celebrated the still-new mascot, the Minuteman.

Some of the university's first community of African-American students at the Orchard Hill complex, where they lived

the recruitment of more black students and faculty. These weren't new proposals, but the incident brought them urgency and attention; the administration responded with what the Afro-American Organization called "honesty and sincerity."

Within a few years, black students had a social meeting place and cultural center in New Africa House, as well as an energized new Afro-American Studies Department staffed by faculty with deep roots in the Civil Rights movement, also housed in New Africa. Meanwhile, CCEBS continued to recruit and foster the education of more black students, as well as Puerto Ricans, Native Americans, and other minorities.

The other front-and-center issue of the day was of course the fighting in Vietnam. Sharply contested at the highest levels of American politics, the war profoundly affected college-age people because they were its soldiers. "I find it difficult to understand," Lederle wrote in response to one parent's letter on the open-house dorm policy, "why [students] can be asked to fight in Vietnam but cannot be trusted to live responsibly in our dormitories." At

one point the *Collegian* ran a feature called Conscription Corner
that answered students' questions about draft status and draft-board
rules. It was the U.S. incursion into Cambodia as well as the killing by the National Guard of four Kent State students in the spring
of 1970 that set off the biggest anti-war demonstrations across the
country—a national student "strike." At UMass, the strike transformed the campus into a kind of political teach-in but was peace-
fully carried out. That same year, in response to student sentiment,
the university dropped academic credit for ROTC, an official course
since the college's founding.

Feminism or "women's lib" also emerged at UMass as the
ratio of female enrollment at last began to rise, especially in graduate programs, with undergrad enrollment gradually approaching
parity in the late 1970s. As late as the fall of 1989, however, 577
tenured full professors were male, but only 68 women shared that
rank. An *Index* of the early 1960s could jokingly refer to a woman
student as "playmate of the month," but by the mid-1970s there
were well-attended pickets against pornography, not to mention
discussions that parsed gender stereotypes and urged the inclusion of women of color and
lesbians in the movement. The Everywoman's Center, one of the first of its kind, opened to
serve women's needs and interests in 1972. Women's athletics burgeoned on campus with
the late-1970s implementation of Title IX, a federal gender-equity law. "Now they say,

New Africa House

Women's soccer team practices on the Boyden
playing fields.

'That was good lacrosse or good field hockey.' It's not just confined to 'that was a good game—for girls,'" one woman athlete in the class of 1976 told the *Index*. "That's one of the best feelings, to have others realize we are highly skilled, serious players."

Civil Rights and feminism, at UMass as at many institutions, initiated a more general breakdown of the assumption that all human experience should conform to a single,

John H. Bracey (left) and Ekwueme Michael Thelwell

After a century of educating only a handful of African-American students, suddenly, in the late 1960s, the University of Massachusetts had more than a hundred black undergrads on its Amherst campus. Though still relatively small in number, the black students at UMass comprised a politically aroused group. In the spring of 1969, after some white fraternity brothers had chased several African-American students to Mills House, their dorm, the black students barricaded themselves inside for protection, ultimately "occupying" the building and presenting the administration with a number of demands. One was for a black studies program.

A detailed proposal for just such a program, drafted by interested faculty, already lay before the faculty senate. The document suggested that studies relating specifically to the black experience would help correct a problem for black students at predominantly white institutions—namely, that their education often left them unable to find "a useful and creative role" in their own communities after graduation. But it also critiqued as intellectually bankrupt any American educational system that confined its perspective to the white middle class: "For the white student, this racial and cultural chauvinism has functioned to defraud him of any sophisticated and accurate vision of his nation's reality. For the black student it has been a damaging and embittering fact of life."

Perhaps partly influenced by the takeover of Mills House (soon renamed New Africa House), the senate approved the new program, and the trustees followed suit on April 22, 1970. A press release sent out that day announced a new major in the area for those intent

privileged model. During the 1970s, the university began offering special services to veterans, students with disabilities, bilingual and foreign students, and older students.

Such reforms both stimulated and resulted from a larger, more diverse student body drawn from a much broader geographical range. By the mid-1960s, more than half of in-state students came from the eastern part of the state. By the fall of 1979,

on pursuing advanced academic work in black studies as well as general courses focusing on African-American life across disciplines including languages, literature, history, anthropology, political science, economics, psychology, music, and fine arts. Not only was this one of the first Afro-American Studies departments in the country, it quickly became one of the best, what founding chair and English professor Ekwueme Michael Thelwell went so far as to call "the most scintillating gathering of black intellectuals anywhere in the world." This was partly due to Thelwell's own connections and recruitment efforts.

Faculty or visiting instructors included working artists—the writers Chinua Achebe, James Baldwin, and Shirley Graham Du Bois; world-renowned jazzmen Max Roach and Archie Shepp; playwright Paul Carter Harrison; dancer Diana Ramos; painter Nelson Stevens—as well as scholars of African-American history, social science, and literature. "These were amazingly strong people," says Professor John H. Bracey, who was teaching at Northern Illinois University near Chicago when he was recruited to join the department at UMass. "You're walking into a situation where, instead of having to build from the bottom up, you're starting with this all-star group."

Bracey says that many early faculty in the W. E. B. Du Bois Department of Afro-American Studies knew each other from "the Movement"—the struggle for civil rights that had gained enormous moral and intellectual energy from the Montgomery Bus Boycott of the 1950s, Martin Luther King's 1963 "I Have a Dream" speech, and the rise in the late 1960s of a Black Power movement that embraced African roots and self-sufficiency.

It was an exciting time for these UMass scholars and their students. Having been accustomed to teaching on an urban campus, Bracey soon found himself savoring the quiet, starlit nights in Amherst. "In those days," he says, "nobody thought in terms of jobs or careers or anything like that. You went where things were interesting. You went where there was some activity."

Chinua Achebe (right) with (from left): Jules Chametsky, Ekwueme Michael Thelwell, and Joseph Duffey

with a combined enrollment of undergraduate and graduate students reaching 24,012, more than 3,000 came from outside the Commonwealth, and 576 came to Amherst from abroad.

It was during and just following its dramatic growth period—a kind of adolescence, as one administrator remarked—that free expression in a diverse community took root as a core value at UMass. "The longstanding elitist pattern of higher education is crumbling," remarked 1970s chancellor Randolph Bromery. "We are seeking out the best minds among minority youth, the poor, the older, the handicapped, women, the retrainable. . . . Our goal is a more responsive and meaningful intellectual community."

EARLY BENEFITS AND CHALLENGES OF GROWTH

The university's explosive expansion did indeed allow for a more diversified intellectual community. In the late 1960s the trustees approved the university's first honors program. Not long after, UMass relinquished its insistence on students' fulfilling "core requirements" in areas such as lab sciences and physical education, but also introduced an array of "interesting and enjoyable courses such as Human Sexuality," as the *Index* put it. These years saw the founding of programs not only in Afro-American Studies but also in Women's Studies, Judaic Studies, Asian Studies, and Linguistics, among others.

The university extended its reach beyond the traditional college student with its University Without Walls, an innovative program allowing older adults to earn a degree through field work and independent study and offering evening and day classes for part-time students through its Division of Continuing Education.

Meanwhile, the university's own growth had taken place in the context of fast-moving developments in higher education across the state as a whole. The Commonwealth founded 10 community colleges during the 1960s. In 1962, a state medical school was founded in Worcester, and an act of the state legislature in 1964 brought into being an urban commuter campus at Boston, at which UMass began to enroll students the following year. The latter two had been envisioned as branches of the Amherst flagship, but in 1970 came dramatic change: State leaders relocated the executive office of this UMass system from Amherst to the state capital, Boston. The system's eastern-based executive would be called the president, while each institution—including the one in Amherst—would have a chancellor as chief administrator.

This was a power shift that advocates of the state college had been fighting since its founding as an agricultural school, when some had proposed folding the land-grant monies into Boston-area institutions. To make the matter still more contentious, trustees short-circuited a search by Amherst faculty to fill the UMass presidency, hiring an MIT political science professor, Robert C. Wood. Wood led certain innovations like the increase in off-campus educational opportunities and defended the university system budget overall. But he was a controversial figure on an Amherst campus accustomed to setting its own policy. In 1971, after trustees rejected Amherst's budget and Wood announced he would transfer $850,000 of its funds to his own office in Boston, UMass Amherst's first chancellor,

UMass Amherst University Without Walls graduates attend the 2011 Commencement.

Oswald Tippo, quit. Tippo, who had been provost at Amherst since 1964, said, "I guess I've been in administration too long."

On the other hand, Amherst securely retained its status as the state's lead academic institution. The new system of co-equal campuses freed it from the responsibility to be all things to all people. And its remoteness from the powers that be (and major media) in Boston allowed it to develop a distinctiveness that might not otherwise have been possible.

BUILDING A CITY

The intensive construction campaign of the 1960s and 1970s not only provided urgently needed new facilities but also brought enormous change to the campus environment, vastly increasing its density and altering its aesthetic. Handsome, relatively small Gothic and Georgian brick structures now shared space with Modernist buildings of poured concrete, dramatic in the simplicity of their lines and dominating in scale. In all, the campus gained more than 180 buildings between 1961 and 1980. Among important additions were the Lederle Graduate Research Center (1966), Whitmore Administration Building (1967), Herter Hall (1969), Murray D. Lincoln Campus Center (designed by the renowned Marcel Breuer and completed in 1970), and the Fine Arts Center (1974).

Oswald Tippo, first chancellor of UMass Amherst

For the first time, the campus climbed skyward, with buildings that constituted a sort of rivalry to the Pioneer Valley's natural topography. In 1966, the dorm complex known as Southwest Residential Area gave that quadrant of campus five 22-story towers along with 12 low-rise residence halls and two dining commons in what then-president Lederle called "historically our greatest single effort at sudden physical growth." In the early 1970s, builders erected, at the heart of the UMass campus just near its iconic stone chapel and pond, the tallest library in the country—a 28-story brick high-rise that remains the tallest academic library in the world.

These changes were at least partly in keeping with a 1962 plan by Sasaki, Walker and Associates, consultants hired by the university to help develop a master plan for

Toward the end of the 1930s, Randolph Bromery was a junior at an all-black school in segregated Cumberland, Maryland. Taking him under her wing, Miss Ruth Franklin, an English teacher and neighbor, selected for him some readings from W. E. B. Du Bois's *The Souls of Black Folk*. For the young man it was an exercise in frustration—he found the reading over his head—but also in motivation. He respected Miss Franklin and wanted to do better.

It wasn't until the early 1940s, when Bromery was being trained as a pilot at Tuskegee, Alabama, that a talk at the nearby Tuskegee Institute got him thinking more about Du Bois and, eventually, taking another look at his work. "You have to get his ideas from reading a lot of his writings," he says. "The one thing Du Bois had from the beginning to the end is the pain of segregation. It became obvious to me after a while that segregation was harder on black intellectuals than it was on anybody, because you knew how irrational it was. As an intellectual you're taught to think, and segregation doesn't fit."

A geologist and geophysicist, Bromery was doing some consulting work in Ghana when he first met Du Bois and his wife, Shirley Graham Du Bois. In the early 1970s, several years after Du Bois's death, Bromery ran into his widow again, this time in Cairo. Her lawyer was there talking with her about her late husband's papers, and Bromery's interest was piqued.

Though he initially thought, as many colleagues did, that the papers should go to a historically black college, it soon became clear that those colleges could neither afford them nor dare take them on, considering their reliance on federal dollars—and how controversial a figure Du Bois had become, at the apex of the Cold War, for his communist sympathies.

Although getting the papers ultimately proved a major coup for UMass, at the time some in Amherst were similarly leery. Indeed, Bromery says he received anonymous phone calls warning that the university must not spend a penny of state money either acquiring or cataloguing the papers.

Instead, a group of scholars and administrators put together a plan to use interest from college investments—its own money, in other words—to offer Mrs. Du Bois a

[enclosure]

> Let not the 12 million Negroes be ashamed of the fact that they are the grand children of the slaves. There is no dishonour in being slaves. There is dishonour in being slave-owners. But let us not think of honour or dishonour in connection with the past. Let us realise that the future is with those who would be truthful, pure and loving. For, as the old wise men have said, truth ever is, untruth never was. Love alone binds and truth and love accrue only to the truly humble.
>
> Sabarmati,
> 1st May, 1929.
>
> *M.K. Gandhi*

A letter from Mohandas K. Gandhi to W. E. B. Du Bois is among the more than 100,000 items in UMass Amherst's collection of Du Bois papers.

the campus. The plan eliminated a main path: Olmsted Drive—later Ellis Way—a curving road that had once joined North Pleasant Street at two points with the east side of campus. Some of the imposing new structures, though meeting the exigencies of the day, had a tendency to confuse or even obstruct pedestrian circulation. Perhaps inevitably, given the incredibly rapid build-up, there were serious technical failures, too. Pieces of brick fell from the façade of the grand new $16.5 million library tower, necessitating its

remittance over several years for the papers as well as to pay for their transport and organization. The clincher for Shirley Graham Du Bois may have been Bromery's argument that he would put the papers at the top of the new 28-story library tower, a little more than 60 miles from Du Bois's childhood home in Great Barrington, Massachusetts. "I saw her light up on that," Bromery recalls. "She was an answer to my prayers, and I was an answer to her prayers."

In the end the university acquired materials from Cairo as well as a trove of Du Bois papers kept in New York City by Herbert Aptheker, a Marxist historian who had been all but blacklisted by academia. Notwithstanding his controversial reputation, the University of Massachusetts Press invited Aptheker to draw upon his unique expertise in the field by becoming editor of Du Bois's collected works.

After that, Bromery found many occasions to lunch with Shirley Graham Du Bois at her home in Cairo. Eventually UMass became home for more than 100,000 Du Bois items—including letters, photographs, manuscripts of published and unpublished writings, memorabilia, and audiovisual materials. Thanks to a 2009 grant by the Verizon Foundation and subsequent additional funds from the National Endowment for the Humanities, nearly all of this important collection has been digitized and placed online for the world to read and use.

Randolph Bromery at a student picnic, 1974

It wasn't until 1994, more than 20 years after UMass's acquisition of the papers, that the towering library housing the collection got Du Bois's name. "The Du Bois papers drew attention to the library, and now the library draws attention to the papers and to the university," says Bromery. "I can't describe the feeling that I have after 45 years here [in Amherst], when I walk on the campus and look up at the library and see that name."

Southwest Residential Area around the time of its

completion in 1966

For those with a taste for high stakes and tight deadlines, putting out a daily newspaper is an incomparable thrill. This may have been especially true during the 1970s, a heyday for the communications industry and the big metropolitan dailies, which played a major role in the politics of Vietnam, Watergate, and other events.

At UMass Amherst, meanwhile, the *Collegian* was unmistakably gaining momentum. Having become a daily and picking up the Associated Press wire in the late 1960s, the paper soon attracted to its staff a collection of passionate young newsies eager to question people in high places, break the stories that mattered at UMass, and get that broadsheet to the Student Union by the break of dawn.

"Many times, you go to college and take classes in your field, but the actual practical work is something that you get later," says Keith Bromery, 1971 *Collegian* top editor. "Well, we had the opportunity to get it right there: What is it like to put out a daily newspaper in a responsible way?" The *Collegian* printed plenty of ads and was emphatically a business—one bringing in about $350,000 a year by 1980. Some positions became salaried and, not surprisingly, staffers often were offered great professional opportunities after graduation—in Bromery's case, offers from the *Miami Herald* and *Chicago Daily News*.

In 1970, the *Collegian* provided all-night coverage of "the Whitmore sit-in, the Afro-Am dispute, and the demonstration against Strom Thurmond" and sponsored a student referendum concerning on-campus recruiting. At times editors faced blowback for criticizing the administration (or, in one case, publishing an editorial that used a profane

temporary closure. Most outrageously, a multimillion-dollar heating plant simply never functioned.

The newly built-up Amherst campus of the 1970s decisively replaced the rural or village feeling of the old ag college with a more sophisticated urban character. Indeed the location of dorm complexes (including the eight-story buildings of Sylvan, added in 1971) and parking areas around the perimeter of campus in some ways echoed development patterns around the country, with "bedroom" communities ringing a central core to which commuters traveled for their daytime activities.

People living and working on campus sometimes expressed a certain dismay at these "surroundings of change and anonymity," as the 1968 *Index* put it. But the residential areas quickly became like neighborhoods, developing their own cultures and gathering places. A 1970 *Collegian* called these "tribal areas"—at Southwest, the "horseshoe"; at Orchard Hill, the green in front of the field; and so on. Some even published their own newsletters, such as the *Orchard Hill Hobbit* and the *Central Voice*. In the mid-1980s, the college yearbook described special local areas for springtime sunning: "Beaches pop up all over campus," it said. "For example, Southwest Horseshoe becomes Southwest Beach, while the open area in Central becomes Gorman Beach."

word to describe then-president Richard Nixon). Columns could start intense editorial-page volleys.

Leaving aside content, producing the paper was no small undertaking. Film had to be developed and photos printed, hard copy laid out by hand in mock-up pages, and all of it loaded into a car to be driven to a commercial printer some 30 miles to the east of campus. Editors spent most of every weekday in the *Collegian* offices; some worked late into the night.

In 1975, one editor crashed his car three miles from the printer but got out and ran the distance with the next day's paper. Staffers made their deadlines during the blizzard of 1978, and in 1979 they watched their February back-to-school issue come off the presses at three in the morning.

If demanding, the work was also exciting and convivial. The *Collegian*, wrote one editor, Fran Basche, in 1980 "has caused grade averages to drop, romances to bloom and die; it has molded reporters, lawyers, cartoonists, graphic technicians, photographers, business success and politicians out of UMass graduates."

One recruitment ad of the same era captured both the humor and the spirit of campus journalists like Basche: "Hate your roommate?" it said. "Join the *Collegian* and you'll never have to see them again."

The banner of an early issue of the *Daily Collegian* from 1971 (top); *Collegian* personnel in the 1980s ready to take personal ads (bottom)

As for the bulked-up mass of *people* at the university—more students, more faculty and staff, more administrators—that could be overwhelming, too. Students sometimes grumbled about crowded dorms, long lines to buy books, and oversubscribed classes. In 1970 the yearbook frankly described registration as "hell week," reserving special animus for newly computerized systems: "'Do not fold, spindle or mutilate obviously does not apply to student nerves.'"

But overall, the fact that the UMass community now constituted a small city accrued to the benefit of its members. For one thing, they enjoyed the services and opportunities afforded by urban scale. By 1980, the campus boasted quite an assortment of businesses and co-ops. The Blue Wall, Top of the Campus, Earthfoods (its philosophy: "to nourish ourselves better by respecting our bodies and the ecosystem"), People's Market, Quickie Lunch, the Candy Counter, and the University Store all occupied the Campus Center alone. There were co-ops providing products or services related to bicycles, photography, sports, and stereos. There was even a campus credit union. The *Collegian* had gone daily in the late 1960s, and become a quite professional organ of news and opinion. UMass had a student radio station in WMUA (in addition to the public radio station WFCR broadcasting from the campus). In 1980 the Fine Arts Center, which had opened five years earlier, hosted members of the Kiev Ballet and Bolshoi Theater while campus rock concerts included the Talking Heads and Jerry Garcia. The student health service, organized in the early 1930s to deal with such crises as epidemics of influenza and polio, opened an 88-bed infirmary in 1962 with a vastly expanded program including psychological services. The bus system that began as a campus circulator had become UMass Transit, then the largest no-fare mass transit system in the country, which carried students to nearby communities and to the campuses of the Five College Consortium.

Student manager Dan Barowy (left) and DJ Mark Gardner in the WMUA radio studio; at work in the People's Market (right)

"UMass Tenures Bowles, Other Radical Economists." So ran an April 9, 1973, headline—not in the *Daily Collegian*, but the *Harvard Crimson*.

UMass's gain, you see, had been Harvard's loss. At least, some people saw it that way. The mid-1970s began a decade of tumult, intrigue, animosity, and always stimulating intellectual debate and exchange, in UMass Amherst's economics department. That's when the so-called radical package headed by Samuel S. Bowles landed in Amherst.

In a controversial decision in late 1972, Harvard had denied tenure to the popular and talented but politically radical Bowles, prompting Dean Alfange, UMass chair of economics, to make him an offer. Alfange was trying to give this unorthodox perspective—which among other things critiqued economic inequality and imperialism—more weight in the department. But Bowles wanted to come to UMass only if he could be assured of entering a collegial atmosphere with at least a few other scholars engaged in like-minded pursuits.

The result was that UMass snapped up Bowles as well as Harvard's Herbert M. Gintis, draining that department of the radical junior faculty who had drawn enthusiastic grad students. "Research and meaningful teaching are hard to carry on in isolation," Harvard's sole remaining radical economist forlornly told the *Crimson*.

Samuel Bowles, 1974

UMass, meanwhile, also hired Richard Wolff and Stephen Resnick, two radical economists from City College of New York, and a grad student from UMass itself, Richard Edwards. This "transformed a department that had been essentially driven by a single paradigm"—nonradical neoclassical economics—"into one in which at least four distinct paradigms came into juxtaposition," according to Donald Katzner, who chaired the department from 1975 to 1980 and has written a book on the period.

Any number of internecine tenure battles, faculty departures, and grad student uprisings ensued, Katzner said in an October 2011 lecture at UMass. So intense were these contests that in 1976 it was thought necessary to draw a line in the sand: 40 percent of the faculty would be "radical," 60 percent "nonradical," and each faction would make its own personnel decisions.

"There were times when I thought the department was going to come apart, but it never happened," said Katzner, not a radical himself. "In the end everyone pulled together and began to appreciate and to some extent even enjoy one another's work and company. Intellectual discussions across boundaries became commonplace and productive."

Over time, the hard line separating radicals from nonradicals blurred; mainstream economics co-opted some of the radicals' issues while the radicals themselves moved closer to the mainstream. In 1994 the department dropped its formal separation of the groups. UMass economics, said Katzner, "has matured into a sort of conscience on the Left for the economics profession at large, and is unlikely to give up that role any time soon."

What's more, almost all of these services were provided in part by students, as volunteers or even as paid staff. This gave UMass undergrads unparalleled opportunities for professional training as broadcasters and print journalists, talent bookers and event planners, caterers and waitpersons, bus drivers and transit dispatchers. This was something you couldn't get at any small liberal arts college.

The size of the student body also made it possible to gather enough people to organize a club around just about any interest one might name, from square dancing to scuba diving to parachuting; by the mid-1970s there were 26 fraternities and sororities; by the mid-1980s, there was Zulu Women's Frisbee, Friends of the Renaissance, and the Dyslexic Student Organization. The intramural sports program, begun in 1949, flourished on the strength of increasing numbers, offering a great variety of team sports and classes, gaining, as the 1980s wore on, programs in then-atypical activities like water polo and fencing.

Intercollegiate athletics also took on more variety (with sports like skiing, cross-country, wrestling, golf, tennis, and lacrosse)—and, at times, great excitement. The apogee: the 1969–70 and 1970–71 basketball seasons, when Julius Erving (already carrying the nickname "Dr. J") displayed his thrilling virtuosity in the intimate enclosure of Curry Hicks Cage. "Rage in the Cage" was a fitting description for these contests, the venue always packed with riveted—and roaring—UMass fans. Lines would form by four o'clock in the afternoon for an 8:00 PM game. Often the Cage would lock its doors by 4:30, so dining commons provided attendees with "Cage survival kits" containing a sandwich, fruit, chips, and a drink. "The Cage was the best place in New England," Coach Jack Leaman, who served from 1966 to 1979, would recall. "It was an intimidating court." Even at a special three-day holiday tournament at New York City's Madison Square Garden in January 1971, all eyes were on UMass and the talented junior forward known for his acrobatic playing style.

That same year, after smashing college records in scoring and rebounding, Erving left UMass for professional play (he would return to complete his degree through the University Without Walls in 1986). "The day the *Collegian* ran the headline 'Erving Signs ABA Pact' the UMass basketball program died a little," lamented the *Index*. "However, it would be selfish for us to expect Julius to remain at UMass when such a lucrative alternative presented itself."

Varsity football had its winning seasons, too, and certainly enjoyed its traditional status as centerpiece of communal events like Homecoming. Under Coach Vic Fusia, the Fighting Redmen, as they were called at the time, won the Yankee Conference football league two years in a row in 1963 and 1964 and were invited to play in post-season bowls. The team accepted in the latter year, flew to Orlando for the game, and was narrowly defeated by the East Carolina Pirates. In 1976 the team finished second in the conference. Games were sometimes televised; in fact in 1976 Coach Dick MacPherson expressed indignation that ABC chose to air an Ivy League game, Harvard versus Brown, instead of the Yankee Conference clash between UMass and New Hampshire.

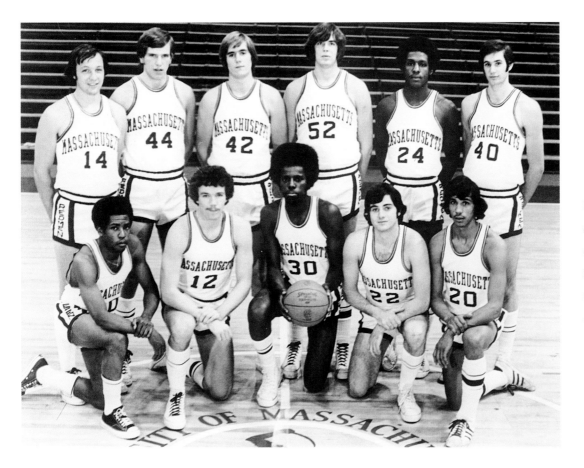

UMass varsity basketball has given a start to numerous NBA stars. For example, the 1973–74 team boasted Al Skinner (front row, center). His team mate, Rick Pitino (at Skinner's left), went on to coach college basketball.

Women's crew, ca. 2003

END OF AN ERA

The post-war boom—that sudden surge in population as well as in the American economy—brought great bounty to the University of Massachusetts and gave it a daunting job to perform. The boom shaped the institution. Then it came to an end.

By the mid-1970s, a seemingly boundless prosperity had given way to an oil crisis, slowdown in productivity growth, and stagnating wages set against spiraling inflation.

In the fall of 1975, a state fiscal meltdown in Massachusetts quickly became a crisis on the Amherst campus, with news of budget cuts and tuition hikes leading students to protest with "a vigor unseen since the sixties," according to the *Index*. The principle at stake: providing "a valuable education to those who could not afford the high cost of private education." Running on an interim budget allocated monthly by the legislature, UMass enacted a hiring freeze. The first week in October, dozens of administrators including UMass Amherst chancellor Randolph Bromery gave up their salaries to pay other employees.

In November, the legislature finally approved a belt-cinching budget for the university. Dorm counselors would not receive their accustomed tuition waivers. Teaching and research jobs for graduate students would face cutbacks. Library equipment would go unrepaired. Student nurses that year protested an announcement that their number would be cut by 50 percent.

In a commencement address that spring, senior Michael Kneeland struck a doleful note that no doubt resonated with much of his audience: "Today," he said, "many of us will leave the graduation line only to join the unemployment line."

The lean years continued. Flat faculty salaries led in early 1977 to the establishment of a union representing UMass Amherst and UMass Boston faculty. The vote to certify the Massachusetts Society of Professors (under the auspices of the Massachusetts Teachers Association) came only after several years of campaigning and three votes; the faculty had been sharply divided, with some arguing that unionization would undermine the meritocracy that rewarded some faculty over others. Negotiations for a first contract ended in the fall of 1978 with increased pay for faculty (though the raises did not altogether make up for recent losses due to inflation) as well as money for educational materials and the like. The creation of the faculty union built on the tradition of what would become one of the most unionized campuses in the United States.

The demographic tsunami of the post-war years required the university to hustle not only as it advanced, but also as it receded. By the early 1980s, administrators were thinking about the implications of a precipitous drop in the college-age population. "Demographic and economic trends," an internal publication warned, "indicate clearly that a sound enrollment management plan for the next decade is a necessity, not a luxury." These trends

Fresh from helping to integrate Minnesota public schools, Norma Jean Anderson came to the UMass School of Education in 1979 and, as associate dean of Student and Alumni Affairs, began bringing in new people. Within two years, fully half the 700 graduate students admitted to the school were people of color, and one-half were women.

At least one aspiring scholar Anderson recruited also happened to be famous: Bill Cosby. He earned a doctorate in education at UMass in 1976, as did his wife, Camille, in 1992.

"I am especially indebted for [Anderson's] faith in my doing graduate work," Bill Cosby wrote in the acknowledgments of his dissertation, "to the extent that she traveled to New York to personally recruit me into the graduate program." At the time, Cosby was already a well-known comedian and television presence.

His dissertation spoke to a rising public concern about the medium that had made him a celebrity: the effects on children of the violence and racial stereotypes depicted in kids' television programming. Cosby focused on three new shows—*Sesame Street*, *The Electric Company*, and *Fat Albert and the Cosby Kids*—that would become classics, helping to educate a generation in the three Rs and shape new attitudes about race, gender, and urban life. Cosby was directly involved in the latter two shows.

Students protesting
budget cuts, mid-1980s

He pointed out that much TV aimed at kids—cartoons, for example—
was replete with violence that was "used to entertain, to evoke laughter. Children could see human beings running into doors, cars driving into brick walls,
explosives going off in people's pockets, someone being shot, run over, hit with
a heavy instrument, but no blood was ever shed. People never died; they all
recovered."

Sesame Street, Cosby wrote, not only avoided this casual violence but also
was the first show actually to teach young children something useful. It gave
instruction in number and letter recognition, concepts of space and time, logical
relationships, and reasoning skills. And it did so against the backdrop of a city
block lined with brownstones and garbage cans that was quite unfamiliar to most
viewers. It shined a positive light on the ethnically diverse people who occupied
Sesame Street. The show, Cosby wrote, demonstrated that TV *could* be educational without sacrificing the pleasures of entertainment. "Sunny day," went the
theme song, "Everything's A-OK."

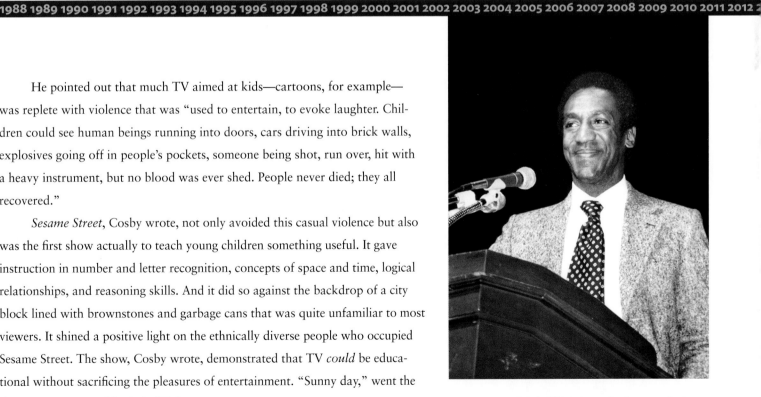

Bill Cosby (Ed.D. '76), wrote his dissertation for the
School of Education on children's television.

A few strokes of the pen in 1977 brought the Massachusetts Society of Professors into being.

suggested that by 1994, Massachusetts would be graduating 44 percent fewer young people from its high schools than it had in 1978.

CULTURE CHANGE

Along with economic and demographic changes—maybe in part because of them—came another culture change among American youth and at UMass in particular. Students abandoned bellbottoms and scoop-necked t-shirts for broad-shouldered blazers and big hair. With jobs scarcer, they became much more interested in securing gainful employment after graduation. It was, in a way, just another swing in the pendulum of public sentiment that had long alternated between a desire for an intellectually and spiritually enlarging "liberal" education and one that would ready the student to make a living.

The humanities lost prestige (and students) to subjects like computer science, engineering, and business. In the 1980s, even as fiscal strain began to ease, yearbooks would increasingly refer to the importance of preparing for the so-called real world. There was less urgency about changing that world and greater preoccupation with getting ahead in it. As one student put it in 1980, education would determine "how we function within our society and the world, and how we make that society and the world function for us."

Among some administrators who had been through the intergenerational shocks of preceding years, the relief was palpable. Dean of Students William Field called 1980 graduates "relaxed skeptics" and "more satisfying students" than those of the late 1960s and early 1970s. "The class members I got to know were open and thoughtful and willing to discuss issues with me with less stridency or certainty than characterized earlier classes," he wrote. "Civility" became the watchword on campus; UMass Amherst chancellor Henry Koffler dubbed 1982 a "Year Toward Civility" to encourage mutually respectful conduct on campus, and founded the Chancellor's Commission on Civility in Human Relations. Meanwhile, far from being intimidated or frustrated by the technological explosion of the latter twentieth century, students of the 1980s made it function for them, as it were. They began bringing their own personal computers to school and enjoying the convenience of the campus's first ATMs.

Population changes dovetailed with the new efficiency-oriented management style that was the becoming the order of the day. "When you build fast and in large numbers, you run into difficulties," UMass system president David C. Knapp said as the 1980s dawned. "And that's what the state did for the last twenty years at UMass." The task now, he said, was to "squeeze that capacity," a job that would require facing down the state's entrenched constituencies and "five million influence brokers." Likewise Koffler, as incoming chancellor at UMass Amherst, identified a need to maintain "absolute insistence on quality performance as a requisite for the allocation of resources to individuals as well as units." "Too many people," Koffler emphasized, "are looking backward with nostalgia to the period of rapid growth, rather than forward with expectations for the challenges of the future."

Chancellor Henry Koffler and his wife, Phyllis, ca. 1982

STEERING THE FLAGSHIP

As it happened, the Massachusetts economy bounced back rather dramatically during the 1980s. UMass thrived along with it, though enrollment stabilized and even tailed off a little, and two decades of vigorous construction activity came to a halt.

More importantly, during the 1980s, the public university began slowly to wean itself away from near total dependency on the state appropriations that, as the decade began and again as it closed, had proven subject to abrupt downshifts. Between 1986 and 1991, for example, though UMass Amherst's total operating budget grew a little, state appropriations fell by millions of dollars, made up for largely by corporate and other grants, and philanthropic gifts. UMass alumni kicked into gear during this decade. By the mid-1980s, they had launched a first-of-its-kind targeted capital fund drive to improve teaching and lab facilities in the School of Engineering, which prompted organizing as an official non-profit within the University of Massachusetts Alumni Association.

The university also increasingly drew its resources from students and their families. Double-digit-percentage tuition-and-fees hikes for in-state students came three years running at both the beginning and end of the 1980s. By the early 1990s, in a "peer" study looking at 36 universities similar in size and mission, UMass campuses topped the list in reliance on student sources of revenue. By then, going to UMass for a year cost 40 percent of state per capita income, the highest rate since World War II.

Through the 1980s, UMass Amherst battled for its flagship status by cultivating excellence in faculty, research, and outreach activities—and by vying for more of the state's higher-achieving students. During the 1970s students' average SAT score had fallen, as had the percentage of those who gave academic reputation as a reason for attending UMass. But from 1981 to 1982 alone, the percentage of freshmen who said academic excellence was a reason for choosing the school rose from 43.3 percent to 57.7 percent. In 1980, the average high school rank of UMass undergrads had been 31, rising to 27 by 1990. Average SAT scores of entering freshmen likewise climbed during the 1980s. The university meanwhile implemented a general education curriculum, a set of requirements aimed at ensuring that no undergrad would leave UMass Amherst without sound communication and analytical skills and exposure to a range of disciplines.

Given how hard they were working—and what they were paying for their education—some UMass students began to rebel against a reputation the school had developed as not just a place of free expression but a rather wild and woolly "party school." They wanted to raise the university's profile in part because they wanted their degrees to bring the respect they thought they'd earned—a sense of indignation hearkening back to Aggie days when students studying botany or entomology, for example, were chagrined by M.A.C.'s reputation as the "cow college." In 1987, one industrious double major in history and engineering told the *Index* she endorsed the recent raising of the drinking age to twenty-one, and was "offended" by the idea that UMass was in any way lax. "I chose UMass over Harvard for my undergraduate education," she said.

To be sure, UMass Amherst's tradition of ardent activism continued, taking on the issues of the day. Take Back the Night marches rallied support against sexual violence; demonstrations for gay rights and the opening in 1985 of the Stonewall Center, which provides advocacy and education to support them, have done much to raise awareness

"This year," yearbook editors wrote in the spring of 1987, "the *Index* sponsored a Twister tournament in response to an identity crisis. Twister was the *Index*'s way to prove that UMass can come together to have a good time without violence."

Emblematic, perhaps, but this Twister-mobile offered a poor surface for play.

The previous autumn, the campus had been the scene of a racial brawl that attracted widespread media attention. The fight occurred in October 1986, after the last World Series game, and pitted predominantly white Boston Red Sox fans against largely African-American New York Mets fans. Several white students were sentenced on charges ranging from riot to assault and battery.

Critical official reports were issued, demonstrations held, and colloquia presented—heavy motivation for a round of Twister, the silly game in which participants reach and bend around one another to touch colored dots on a mat. And, the *Index* was onto something: The Twister game *did* prove to be a fun, unifying event—and it set a new world record for the largest Twister game in history. On a spring day, as the chapel clock struck one in the afternoon, 4,160 UMass folks responded in unison to the first call of the game: "Right foot, red." It went on for some three hours, until finally a single twister remained in the contest, senior Alison Culler.

The Twister game of 1987 set a precedent for other record-bursting unity events at UMass. Happily none of these were preceded by acrimonious clashes, but they did serve a purpose with their lighthearted fun.

of LGBT issues. Students came out to protest apartheid in South Africa as well as racism much closer to home, including a march in response to a racially motivated attack on a black student after the 1986 World Series. Probably the most visible case of collective action likewise came in the 1986–87 school year, when a roving protest against CIA recruitment on campus occupied first the Whitmore administration building, then Munson. It eventually drew some seven hundred people, including Abbie Hoffman, first made famous for his role in protests during the 1968 Democratic National Convention, and Amy Carter, daughter of the former president.

But as the turn of another century approached—and across the country the cost of a college education skyrocketed—the challenge at UMass Amherst would be to safeguard a tradition even more fundamental to its mission. How could the university continue its bid for excellence, while staying true to the spirit of Levi Stockbridge, the Hadley farmer who had set the first M.A.C. students to clearing the land around South College? Addressing the college's inaugural class of local farmboys, Stockbridge had insisted the Commonwealth's institution of higher learning must remain accessible to the people, "dispensing its privileges equally to high & low, the rich and poor, the foreign and native born."

In autumn 2010 UMass Amherst got together to shape 650 sheets of seaweed, 200 pounds of sushi rice, and enormous quantities of avocado, cucumber, and Alaskan crab into the longest California roll ever created (thus relieving the University of California Berkeley of its record). The 90-minute project fostered "a sense of community," explained UMass's vice chancellor for student affairs. The next year it was the largest stir-fry ever—with more than four thousand pounds of vegetables and chicken.

"Our goal was to do more than just set a new world record," said Ken Toong, executive director of Auxiliary Enterprises at UMass Amherst. "We did it while also supporting sustainability and promoting healthy eating as we welcome our students back to school."

On May 2, 1987, the massive Twister Tournament on campus challenged more than 4,000 students to rethink certain positions, at least momentarily.

1990 UMass graduate students unionize

1991 Richard D. O'Brien becomes chancellor

1993 David K. Scott replaces O'Brien

· Mullins Center completed.

1996 Campaign UMass launched

· Silvio O. Conte National Center for Polymer Research completed

1999 Commonwealth College (later renamed Commonwealth Honors College) created

2001 Marcellette G. Williams assumes chancellorship, becoming first woman chancellor at UMass Amherst

2002 John Lombardi becomes chancellor

2003 UMass Amherst Foundation created

2005 Library's Learning Commons opens

2006 Central Heating Plant dedicated

2007 Thomas W. Cole, Jr., takes on chancellorship

2008 Robert C. Holub replaces Cole

UMASS

THE UNIVERSITY OF MASS

2009 UMass Amherst stakeholders issue "Framework for Excellence"

2010 Students establish first food-producing "permaculture" garden

2011 Holub announces move by football team into Mid-American Conference

- Community College Connection launched

- UMass Innovation Institute created

2012 Kumble R. Subbaswamy named chancellor

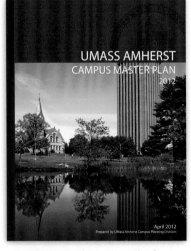

- UMass designers submit master plan for campus development

2013 UMass Amherst celebrates sesquicentennial

RISING

HUSETTS AMHERST AT 150

A newcomer to a university as significant as UMass Amherst
needs to walk the place from one end to the other,
through the buildings and along the well-traveled and not-so-often-used paths.
Such a walk provides a hint of what the place is, has been, and can be.

—Former Chancellor John Lombardi, 2012

INTO THE FUTURE

Continuity, Change, Sustainability

T HINK OF THE FIRST CLASS OF 30-SOME LOCAL FARMBOYS WHO PULLED UP TO SOUTH COLLEGE IN HORSE-DRAWN CONVEYANCES IN THE AUTUMN OF 1867. THE CAMPUS THEY HAD SURVEYED ON THEIR JOURNEY WAS ABANDONED FARMLAND THEY THEMSELVES WOULD BE EXPECTED TO CLEAR AND DRAIN. THEIR PROJECT WAS TO HELP LAUNCH THE COMMONWEALTH'S FIRST PUBLIC COLLEGE. IF THEY COULD SEE INTO THE FUTURE, WHAT WOULD THEY MAKE OF THE UNIVERSITY OF MASSACHUSETTS AMHERST AT ITS ONE HUNDRED FIFTIETH BIRTHDAY?

DATELINE 2013: UMASS TODAY AND TOMORROW

They might first of all be astonished that such a seemingly tenuous venture had not only endured but grown into a scholarly community of tens of thousands, living and working in hundreds of buildings and generating more than 6,700 undergraduate and graduate degrees in the 2011–12 academic year alone. They'd be amazed by the technology that allows these community members to be in touch with one another and the world instantly and at any hour of the day or night. The first students of Massachusetts Agricultural College would surely marvel that the Industrial Revolution they were witnessing with excitement but also a certain dismay had come full circle, with today's UMass committed to a more sustainable, earth-friendly way of life. They would be astounded by the university's research capabilities in areas that to them would have seemed downright otherworldly—things like nanotechnology and biofuels. And, chances are, they would be intrigued by today's classes in sustainable agriculture, biotechnology, and animal genetics.

George and Charlie, two cloned cows

Danielle Henderson proudly holding her Olympic gold medal

Danielle Henderson '99 remembers UMass Amherst sports fans as something really special. How could she not? By her junior year, they'd recognize and stop the record-smashing pitcher from Commack, New York, as she made her way across campus and even around town. "Aren't you Danielle?" people would ask.

"The fans really showed a lot of love and that's what made it a great place," says Henderson. That's saying a lot, considering the truly heady times Henderson encountered just after graduating. That summer, she competed with the U.S. National Softball Team, which won the gold medal at the Pan American Games. The next summer, she flew to Sydney, Australia, to play for the United States in the 2000 Olympic Games. The team came home with gold.

The truth is, Henderson herself helped create the sort of UMass fans she so appreciated—the ones who go wild for a women's sport like softball and not just for those traditional crowd rousers, football and men's basketball.

Recruited by longtime UMass softball head coach Elaine Sortino, Henderson had what the coach called "a God-given wrist snap" and plenty of drive. Under Sortino she worked on honing those skills every day. "A lot of coaches just kind of let you play," says Henderson. "She had this way of letting you know you had to do everything to the best of your ability, work as hard as you possibly could."

The crowds were modest Henderson's freshman year. But by her second year the women's thrilling play was pulling them in. "There was a big moment the first time we won

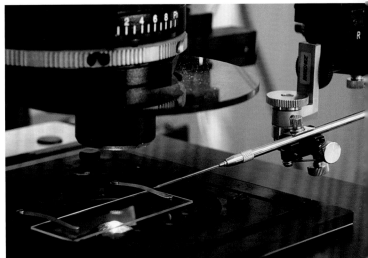

Mostly broad-minded in their values, those Massachusetts farmboys would be impressed that half the students of the twenty-first-century university are women, and one in five is nonwhite.

A researcher working in a lab at the Cranberry Experiment Station (left); laser confocal fluorescence microscope in the Keck Nanostructures Lab, Conte Polymer Science Building (right)

regionals and got to go to the college World Series," she says. "That really stands out. It was a come-from-behind thing; we were in the losers' bracket. And that's when the fan base really started to grow. Afterward we went to Rafters, a little sports pub on the edge of campus, and people stood up and gave us a standing ovation. They were standing on the tables clapping for us!" Junior year brought another regionals victory. "We had the baseball and lacrosse teams there. These guys were cheering for us, getting the crowd going. Whenever there was a strike-out the guys would get down and do push-ups."

In her junior and senior years, Henderson led the nation in strikeouts per seven innings. She capped her UMass athletic career by winning the Honda Award for the nation's best softball player. Following Henderson's Olympics turn, UMass retired her number, 44; she was the first woman in UMass history to be so honored.

After assistant coaching at UMass, then giving private lessons for some years, Henderson became a pitching coach at Ohio State in 2010. But she keeps tabs on the team to which she gave the passion and momentum of her college days. "The sustained success of the program keeps people coming out," she says. "Senior Day, spring 2012, they had a sold-out crowd." In that day's doubleheader, the Minutewomen swept Charlotte, 3–1 and 8–0.

UMass Women's Varsity Softball team

And if the founders of what would become UMass could survey the scene today? Well, they'd be witnessing the triumph of an idea they cherished: that going to college is a useful and rewarding experience not just for well-to-do young men but for everyone. Unlike local farm families of the nineteenth century, no American today can afford to scoff at the importance of a college education, an essential tool for making it in the twenty-first-century economy. But surely M.A.C.'s founders would also whistle in astonishment at the

Each year nearly 40,000 people tour the UMass Amherst campus, with an additional 15,000 visitors a year attending open houses, one in the autumn for prospective students and 10 in the spring for accepted students. April is the busiest month for visitors, as accepted students make their decisions about where they'll spend their college years. It's the job of UMass Amherst's 40 student tour guides to introduce visitors to UMass, show them around, answer their questions, and, in the process, try to pass on a little Minuteman spirit. Here, some perspective from experienced tour guide Daniel Burke '12.

You really have to bone up on UMass to prepare to be a student tour guide. What did you learn that surprised you?

Most students here don't understand that UMass began as Massachusetts Agricultural College. It's great to go to the greenhouses, where it becomes clear, but otherwise you wouldn't necessarily have a sense of the university's agricultural past. You also feel it when you leave campus by the back roads down to the mall—it's farmland.

The UMass Amherst campus is huge—1,450 acres in all—and pretty hilly. Do people get worn out on your 75-minute tour?

People do sometimes ask if they can take the bus! But our campus is laid out in three concentric circles. People want to see the academic buildings, a typical classroom. They want

price even working families pay to grab hold of that tool, at least until they compared it to similar universities in New England. While the average UMass student leaves school with some $25,000 in educational debt, that is still significantly lower than what students face at comparable institutions. "So happy you're graduating," one family quipped to their child in a congratulatory ad in the *Index*. "We are out of money."

to take pictures of the library. People want to see social areas. We point out the Japanese elm by South College to emphasize international studies, because that was given to us by our sister college in Japan, the first Japanese elm tree planted on American soil. All this is in the central ring of campus. The next ring out is where the residence life is, and we take them to see a dorm. But the tour focuses on that inner ring. We have specific stops and we're given about six to seven hours of material, so it's at the tour guide's discretion how to boil it down to 75 minutes.

What concerns do visitors express about UMass?
The most consistent concern that comes up, without a doubt, is size. UMass is the largest institution in New England. We usually talk about how, because of the layout of the campus, it quickly feels so much smaller. There's a lot of acreage but the parts you use every day are not so big. Anybody can find the right niche.

What kinds of questions do prospective students ask?
They often ask questions geared toward student life and campus activities. And that's an area where size is a big advantage. It's because we have so many people that there are so many activities. We have things like the Mullins Center, a big venue that gets a lot of big-name bands coming through here.

On tours you take people through the Student Union and you can tell them, "We have the largest student newspaper in New England and it's very good. Go ahead and take a copy." Here you can study journalism but you can also write for a quality daily paper. Or you can work for the radio station and earn your FCC license. I'm an accounting major and in one course in the spring we do taxes for anyone in the local area who makes under $57,000. It's a great way to use what you learned in the classroom.

What do parents want to know?
They'll ask about academics and how the degree plays in the job market. I interned last summer with Ernst & Young, a major accounting firm. Interning there I thought the UMass students worked the hardest; maybe we had something to prove not going to one of the private schools, but the UMass students really did stand out. That's when you feel proud of where you come from.

THE PEOPLE'S UNIVERSITY: WHO PAYS?

In many ways, the question hearkens back to the earliest days of the state's public college: Will the Commonwealth itself take ownership of the institution on behalf of its citizens and pledge to support it? This question has been far from settled at various points in UMass's history, but this time it arises in the context of a nationwide disinvestment in public higher education.

In Massachusetts over the last 20 years, successive waves of economic recession and aggressive tax cutting have resulted in a dramatically reduced role for the state in

In October 2010, students, faculty, and alumni walked 100 miles, from Pittsfield to Boston, urging Massachusetts legislators to reverse the state's disinvestment in public colleges and universities. Senator Rosenberg greeted and addressed them at the rally in front of the State House on October 7.

Stanley Rosenberg, one of UMass Amherst's many "nontraditional" undergraduates—he ultimately earned his bachelor's degree through the Continuing Education program—went on to distinguish himself as a staunch campus ally in state government. Elected first to the Massachusetts House of Representatives in 1986 Rosenberg began his State Senate career in 1991. Among other important contributions, he has ably promoted bond bills to finance the major capital improvements needed to make the Amherst campus "sparkle," as he puts it. This work helped bring to fruition the Mullins Center, the Integrated Sciences Building, and the Silvio O. Conte National Center for Polymer Research, among others.

You grew up in foster care in the Boston area, presumably without a lot of money for college. How did you get to UMass Amherst?

I was a reasonably good student, and a number of the teachers took an interest in me. They encouraged me to think about college. I did not have resources. I got into a number of [private Massachusetts] colleges, but UMass was the only one that offered financial aid. The rest said that I was on my own, so it was impossible for me to attend those schools. UMass was my only and best option!

And I had the experience at UMass that I needed to have, because I'm an experiential learner and there was a lot of flexibility in programs. I was able to participate in the BDIC [Bachelor's Degree with Individual Concentration] program and then went on to Continuing Education. It was 10 years from admission to my degree, but it was a great time.

supporting UMass Amherst. During the college's exuberant growth period of the 1960s, the Commonwealth supplied more than 80 percent of its budget, but by 2012 that portion had dropped to less than half. The loss has been made up partly by private contributions and money from government agencies, non-profits, and corporations, which generally go toward specific activities or research. But the gap has been filled mostly by students and their families that the university has committed to helping. In fact, since 2000 the cost to students attending UMass Amherst has more than doubled, just as has the amount distributed among students in financial aid.

Mullins Center

"Extension"—carrying the university's assets to the people of Massachusetts—has been a major part of UMass's mission from the beginning. But there was little effort to stimulate cultural activity across the state until 1973, when you founded the Arts Extension Service, providing all kinds of training for artists and arts organizations. Why was that important?
At UMass I put together a joint major through BDIC in community development and arts administration. I was interested in how the arts contribute to social change. Since I was studying this area and involved in a variety of arts, from band to chorus to musical theater, I was asked by Continuing Education to conceptualize how the university could extend its arts resources to the broader community. We started a series of projects; people could get music lessons or community-based organizations could learn how to manage their community work.

You graduated in 1977. Has the campus become more tolerant since your college days?
America is maturing. There is social change going on all around us, and it's measured in decades and generations, unfortunately, rather than days and weeks. People bring, from their home communities, their experience, their perspectives. Sometimes they bring value systems that need to be challenged. That's part of what a great university can do: help them broaden their experience and perspectives.

Four Chancellor's Personal Hosts escort Senator Ted Kennedy at groundbreaking ceremony for the Integrated Sciences Building.

THE RACE IS ON

One effect of the nationwide shift away from state funding is that in order to fulfill a deeply held commitment to teaching and producing socially valuable research and scholarship, UMass Amherst must compete in a new kind of marketplace—compete for paying students, compete for research dollars, compete for the top-notch faculty who will bring in more grants, and build the state-of-the-art facilities that will attract those faculty and students.

The university has sought to lift its profile on the state and national stage, strengthening itself against future competition. In 2008 the trustees of the UMass system committed themselves to creating "a strong and nationally recognized flagship" in Amherst. Lifting UMass Amherst's profile required, for one, working to recruit high-performing students from across the Commonwealth and beyond. By 1998, the university had increased incoming SAT scores by 10 points a year. Between 2004 and 2011, applications spiked from 17,930 to 32,564, the average SAT score of incoming students rose from 1137 to 1189, and the average high school rank improved from twenty-ninth to twentieth. The university transformed a long-standing honors program into an official Commonwealth Honors College; it opened in 1999 and by the autumn of 2011 had 682 entering students with a combined average SAT score of 1327. That year the university broke ground on a $186.5 million teaching and living complex for the honors college, with four- to six-story buildings arranged around a series of courtyards—a "visible representation of the commitment of this campus to academic excellence," as dean of the college Priscilla Clarkson said.

After leveling off as the Baby Boom ebbed, total undergraduate enrollment rose again, from just over 17,000 in the fall of 1992 to more than 20,000 in the autumn of 2011. In recent years this has been on the strength of increases in students from out of state—whose ranks swelled from around 3,400 in 2005 to 4,341 in 2011—as well as those who hail from Massachusetts. In 2006, the legislature decided to let UMass Amherst

Priscilla Clarkson, Dean of Commonwealth Honors College

Acceptance packages at the admissions office prior to being mailed

In 1962, Canadian native Fergus Clydesdale came to UMass to earn a doctorate, which he followed in 1967 by becoming an assistant professor in the Department of Food Science. Soon the popularity of his courses was packing lecture halls and earned him the university's Distinguished Teaching Award in 1972. Clydesdale rose in the ranks to serve as department head for 20 years, and during that time he published hundreds of research articles and wrote or edited some 20 books.

In the 1970s, his undergraduate course was called "The Struggle for Food," by which he referred to "the worldwide struggle to get enough food for the rising populations," not just in so-called third-world areas, but right here in parts of the United States. Nevertheless, he scrupulously avoided the political aspects of this issue in order to focus entirely on the science.

Perhaps Clydesdale's attitude and his insistence on keeping the big picture in mind could be characterized best as pragmatic. His espousal of the judicious use of technological developments and methods for processing foods in order to optimize nutritional value and permit long-distance transportation to those most in need sometimes drew criticism. But his attitude is easily explained by his experience in teaching food science. For example, when explaining the oxidation of fats, which often results in foods looking, smelling, and tasting bad, he would ask students: "You've all smelled rotten fish, right? No? No one's smelled rotten fish? You've all seen moldy bread? No again. They have no experience with food, . . . and I think that's because processing and preservation are now being done so well and cheaply."

Another adjective for Clydesdale's outlook is *humane*. Again in the 1970s, the "lifeboat theory" seemed to be gaining credence among a surprisingly sizable group of experts. As he describes it, the idea holds "that there was so much starvation in the world that you only helped those nations that were possible to save. If you let the others in the lifeboat, it would sink." The frightening potential of such sentiments caused him to recognize that what the major food companies were producing offered the far better option.

For many years Clydesdale has been a mover and shaker in national and international food policy, serving on numerous influential advisory boards, including the Dietary Guidelines Committee of the U.S. Department of Health and Human Services, the group that generates the federal government's gold-standard, science-based nutritional-intake guidelines for the American public, on which he served in 2005. He retired from his professorship in 2008 in order to direct the university's Food Science Policy Alliance, a master's program that also brings together government, industry, consumer, and scientific groups concerned with food policy.

Fergus Clydesdale, director of UMass Amherst's Food Science Policy Alliance

Students in a food sciences class practice dicing potatoes.

keep out-of-state tuition rather than send it back to the state's general fund; out-of-state tuition is also significantly higher than in-state charges. So this was partly a strategy for increasing revenue, especially as the dire national recession that began in 2008 took its toll. But it also was meant to attract greater notice to the Amherst campus.

FACULTY: THE BACKBONE OF THE UNIVERSITY

It hardly needs saying that a robustly proportioned, stellar faculty is also vital to raising the university's reputation. Quality has never been lacking in UMass Amherst's teaching corps. UMass offers competitive benefits, a collegial intellectual environment linked to companion institutions in the Five Colleges, and a desirable setting in the Pioneer Valley.

Quantity is another matter. During the 1990s, the number of faculty on campus decreased to the point that tenure-system faculty had dwindled from a high of around 1,200 in the late 1980s to 958 in the fall of 2005.

Students lamented large class sizes and the fact that the adjunct professors and graduate students who were increasingly teaching their classes had a hard time following their work, evaluating it carefully, and giving them recommendations for graduate study or other post-graduate work. One sociology professor said she now had to teach 225 students the same material on the family she'd once taught to a class of 40. "In the class with only 40 students," she said, "I learned the names of all the students. I talked to many of them extensively, both inside and outside the classroom. They got to know one another and found themselves in intense discussions with me as well as the other students." More recently, she recalled, she'd gone to the movies and been stopped by a student who'd recognized her voice—but not her face, as the student sat in the back of the large class.

Such concerns bespoke the seriousness of both faculty and students at UMass. It vividly illustrated their commitment—indeed their longing—to participate in the intergenerational exchange between professor and student that is the backbone of the university experience.

Then, UMass Amherst Chancellor John V. Lombardi committed to the so-called Amherst 250 plan, the five-year goal of which was to reverse the long decline in tenure-track faculty. The plan gained traction during the next few years, but ran smack into the financial crisis of 2008 and stalled. Even so, by 2011–12 the number of tenure-system faculty stood at 993—an improvement, if not as substantial a gain as that envisioned—and UMass leaders remained committed to the goal of increasing the faculty.

UMass graduate students had been among the first in the country to unionize, in 1990, and post-doctoral fellows (people in temporary research posts who already hold a PhD) formed a union in 2010. Together with UMass Amherst's other staff, these academic employees make up the largest unionized workplace in New England. What's more, a grassroots group of faculty, students, and staff based mainly at UMass Amherst rallied friends of higher education across the state and in 2007 formed PHENOM (Public Higher Education Network of Massachusetts), a group that advocates for the enterprise of higher education.

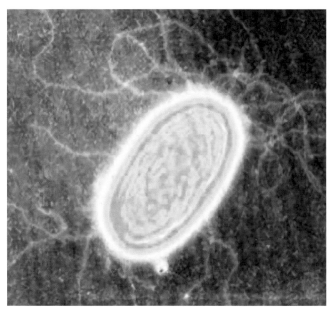

Microbiology professor Derek Lovley (left) at the site on the Potomac River where he discovered the *Geobacter* bacterium (above)

RESEARCH, A STRONG SUIT

Tenure-system faculty, often very accomplished teachers, are also the campus's main producers of research and scholarship—a productivity that in turn is vital to establishing UMass as a top public university.

Although college faculty have been doing research since Levi Stockbridge first developed his famous and best-selling fertilizers in the nineteenth century, UMass Amherst began its climb into the upper echelons of research institutions during the 1980s and 1990s and now stands as one of just a few dozen public universities credited with "very high research activity" by the Carnegie Foundation. Sponsored research grew by a paltry 2 percent annually during the doldrums of the late 1980s and early 1990s, then picked up to a nearly 5 percent annual growth rate in the late 1990s and has really taken off in the twenty-first century. Grant awards grew by some 50 percent during the century's opening decade, reaching $140 million by fiscal year 2011. The majority of those funds come from government, but about 20 percent are split between private non-profits and industry.

UMass Amherst has become well known for leading work in a number of areas—like alternative energies, including microbiologist Derek Lovley's discovery, in the sands of the Potomac River, of the *Geobacter* species of bacteria, capable of "eating" oil-based pollutants and radioactive material. Computer scientist Kevin Fu has developed an international reputation for work making computer systems faster, more secure, and more energy

In 2002, UMass microbiology research associate Thomas Warnick was hiking a few miles east of campus on a trail descending to the Quabbin Reservoir. He stooped to collect a soil sample, as had been the habit of friends and associates of microbiologist Susan Leschine since the 1980s. Indeed, they had collected dozens of samples from all over the world. But it was in this spoonful of soil taken right near Amherst that the scientists hit pay dirt: a microorganism uniquely capable of turning plants into the clean-burning fuel ethanol.

Like so many scienctific discoveries, this one was a case of luck favoring the well prepared. UMass's Leschine had long been studying how microbes decompose biomass— plant material—in the absence of oxygen (when submerged in ponds, for example), a process that represents about 10 percent of carbon turnover on the planet. "Of course, these microbes could possibly convert this biomass to useable products," says Leschine. "That was an obvious implication."

Even so she never imagined that this particular microbe, *Clostridium phytofermentans*, would soon have her and UMass working with patent attorneys and, later, venture capitalists, to try to bring the tiny organism into commercial production and practical, eco-friendly use. Soon it received a catchier name: the Q Microbe, for its origin near the Quabbin Reservoir.

"We had these samples from all around the world and were isolating the bacteria that break down biomass," recalls Leschine. "Most of them were very similar. We had Q isolated, and it appeared to be behaving similarly, but there were some characteristics that were different. And it just became more and more undeniable: It's not just a little bit different."

Left: Thomas Warnick in the lab with students Ayesha Sundaram and Ima Otudor; right: Susan Leschine

Based on its unusual genetic characteristics, Leschine and colleagues named and characterized the bacteria in 2002. But it wasn't until 2005 that they discovered its most outstanding trait—more or less by accident. Warnick had made a mistake preparing the usual medium for testing microbes, putting way too much filter paper made up of cellulose (the main constituent of plant cell walls) in the mulchlike substance. Leschine and Warnick decided to inoculate it with the microbe anyway. "What happened," says Leschine, "is that Q turned the filter paper basically into ethanol. Something that was a mistake turned into a real eye-popper of an experiment."

At that point the university filed a provisional patent application on the microbe. Through further research, Leschine and her colleagues were able to describe its unique properties more fully: It can break down all kinds of widely available plant material including switchgrass, sugarcane, and various constituents of corn. It performs a direct conversion of biomass into ethanol, whereas typically that's a two-part process in which microbes first break down plant material into sugars; then other products like yeasts are used to convert the sugars to ethanol. The Q Microbe process is unusually efficient, with ethanol its main product, far exceeding the amount of byproduct.

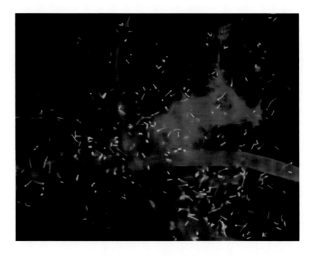

Fluorescence micrograph showing *Clostridium phytofermentans* (Q Microbe) cells (green) growing on paper (blue) as they convert the paper to ethanol

"I wanted to see it actually used," says Leschine. "That doesn't happen unless you go out and beat the bushes." So beat them she did, making the rounds of all kinds of businesses, including multinational oil companies, to gauge their interest in commercializing the "natural biorefinery" UMass had discovered in its own backyard. "This was 2005; gas prices were going up, and there was a lot of talk about renewables," she recalls. In the end though, Leschine once again found her answer very close to home, in the form of four Amherst businessmen. They formed a startup, SunEthanol, later renamed Qteros, and licensed the technology from UMass.

Unfortunately, a third round of venture funding ran aground during the economic tailspin that began in 2008, and key investors decided not to provide additional funding. In 2012, however, a private entrepreneur arranged to purchase the assets of Qteros and intends to continue development of this unique discovery. Interest elsewhere, notably India, may also lead to additional work with the Q Microbe.

So far Qteros has paid hundreds of thousands of dollars to UMass in licensing fees for its patent rights. Leschine has gotten ongoing support for her research. And if the microbe once hidden in the soil near Quabbin Reservoir reaches the market, UMass research will have contributed a link in the chain that leads to solving perhaps the world's most pressing problem: the environmental crisis caused by greenhouse gas emissions.

efficient. In 2011 the campus's Institute for Holocaust, Genocide, and Memory Studies opened on the strength of several personal and institutional gifts; it offers scholars around the world a space to study and teach about the human calamity of genocide. These are just a few examples.

The university has also made a concerted effort to license its discoveries to companies that can bring them to the public—whether it's a potential biofuel like Q Microbe or a pressure vest that's therapeutic for conditions like autism and anxiety. Early in 2012, the team of polymer scientists and a biologist who developed Geckskin, a superadhesive device, made headlines in the science media. "If it's new knowledge produced here at the university," says Mike Malone, vice chancellor for Research and Engagement, "we want

William Hite

The *Boston Globe* once called tenor William Hite "a breathtaking communicator." The *San Francisco Chronicle* remarked that in Henry Purcell's opera *King Arthur* he "lavished the music with considerable eloquence," and the *Sunday Oregonian* credited him with a "commanding but relaxed presence."

By 2002, after more than two decades as a working artist based in Boston, it was clear the man could sing. Using the finely trained instrument of his own voice, he could convey nuance and intensity to just about any audience. But teaching that art to adolescents? That, he very quickly realized, after taking a full-time position as voice instructor at UMass Amherst, is a challenge all its own.

"It's just very complicated," says Hite, 10 years into the job. "Having to work with young students, I really had to think hard about what I do, and then figure out a way to express that to teenagers who have little or no frame of reference. You figure out new ways to express it, and then you meet a new kid who presents a different skill set or learning mode. Not everyone responds the same way. So it's a big growth experience being a teacher."

Teaching an applied art like voice means individual lessons and thus a certain unpredictability. Though Hite does create a syllabus, it's not possible to predict just how each of the 16 students walking through his door every week is going to advance through the academic calendar. The process has to be somewhat "intuitive," he says.

It's a process that draws heavily on Hite's experience as a working artist. "Without the backing of my own study, and the extended study as manifested in my singing career, I would have been hopeless," he says. "What a career brings is all of the perspective of all of the singers I've heard, good and bad; all the performances I've done, successful and less successful; all of the conductors I've run into, and all the repertoire. It's hard to think of an aspect of my career that hasn't informed my teaching."

On the other hand, teaching while singing professionally creates the usual dilemma faced by artists in academia: how to find time to do both well. The academic year more or less coincides with Hite's busy season as a singer, so sometimes it's truly a marathon

Students study exhibits at the Institute for Holocaust, Genocide, and Memory Studies, which opened in 2011.

venture. "Teaching is a vocally tiring thing; it's like six hours of talking," says Hite. "And then if you have to hop on a plane and sing, it's pretty draining."

When he first started teaching, it was always the preparation for performance that fell by the wayside. It was stressful going on stage under those circumstances, even if he always tried to pull the very best performance out of himself. With time and experience he has found a better balance.

In fact, the 2011–12 academic year was particularly rewarding. "I thought I'd sort of mark the tenth anniversary of my being at UMass by being really, really active, and so I created a series of performances on campus," says Hite. He also was invited to sing a couple of particularly choice parts off campus, both leading roles for the tenor.

One was the Evangelist in Bach's *St. Matthew Passion* for the Boston Cecilia, "a big, complicated, very dense sort of virtuosic vocal test," as Hite says. Another exciting gig was the title role in Mozart's opera *La Clemenza di Tito*. This one was full of challenging arias and also stretched Hite's acting skills in playing a ruler "who is endlessly patient and endlessly forgiving and very wise," he says. The venue was Emmanuel Music, the performing arm of Emmanuel Church in Boston, where Hite sang regularly earlier in his career. "For them to invite me back for this prominent role felt like such an honor," he says.

But Hite has been around the block enough times as a freelance artist to understand that the next season could be entirely different. If the upsurge in great opportunities represents a pattern, he says, "I'll take it. If not, I'll take that too."

That's a perspective he brings to teaching, too, one that surely benefits young students setting off on careers of their own. "If your image of your success as a teacher is only wrapped up in how well they do their thing, that's kind of sad," Hite remarks. "Sometimes what they learn is they're not a singer. That's a success. They don't all improve the same amount. But they all grow up. One of the wonderful things about what I do is that I see a lot of 17- and 18-year-olds grow into 21- and 22-year-olds. It's such a period of change. I feel lucky to be part of it."

it to benefit society. The point isn't just to make money in technology transfer. It's to have impact." In 2011 the university opened its UMass Innovation Institute to serve as a gateway between industry and the researchers producing potentially valuable discoveries.

Malone says it's important to remember that only about half the faculty conduct externally sponsored research, and the rest also must produce scholarship—books, articles, works of art—as part of their mission. All of this takes place alongside teaching. "Our main contribution," says Malone, "is our graduates. We are in the education business."

BUILDING FOR A NEW CENTURY

As UMass Amherst entered the 1990s, the vast building that had taken place during its post-war period of rapid expansion had come to an end. Worse, little had been done to plan for the ongoing maintenance and renovation of those many buildings, which were showing their

On September 16, 2010, 57-year-old George N. Parks walked off a field in Cuyahoga Falls, Ohio, after performing with the UMass Minuteman Marching Band he'd led since not long after leaving college himself. These would be his last steps. The legendary band director was having a heart attack. But the energy he brought to every single day would live on in extraordinary ways.

George N. Parks in the late 1970s (above) and around 2009 (opposite)

"George," recalls the band manager at the time (and mellophone player) Caity Bogdan, "is probably the only person who could possibly die in this really tragic and sudden way, and you could still manage to come out of the weekend and feel like you had gotten to see something good about life. A great leader works out a system that's so flawless it can run itself. He had created that system."

The Minuteman Marching Band had made a stop in Ohio en route to Ann Arbor, Michigan, and its most high-stakes performance of the season—a football game between UMass and the University of Michigan, itself the home of a certain classic marching band style. Parks died on a Thursday. The Michigan game was on Saturday. So the band members had a little time "to be with ourselves," says Bogdan, "to celebrate and mourn with each other just what it was that we had lost."

Part of that process involved a determination to go forward. "It was amazing for me to watch," says Bogdan. "From the logistical side there was no stutter whatsoever. On top of that, he had created this group of people who were such a family to each other. We said, 'What he would have wanted is for us to go make an impression, show that we are the best band in the land. He would have wanted us to go to Michigan and just floor everybody.' And so that's what we did."

age. One example: The campus's largest science facility, the Morrill complex, lacked the systems that would allow for the intensive use of chemical-fume hoods. Another: The iconic Old Chapel was closed in 1997 because of structural problems, displacing the university's famed marching band. If the university was to compete in the coming century, the campus would have to look sharp and function as a modern living and research environment.

So beginning in the early 1990s, the university began diverting operating funds to pay for capital projects, in the form of both direct expenditures and debt service for capital borrowing. This launched an aggressive self-financed capital borrowing program through the University of Massachusetts Building Authority, which by 2009 had financed nearly $750 million in current and planned projects. Through these and other funding sources, including state-issued bonds and private donations, during the last 15 years the Amherst campus has undergone its first building boom since the Baby Boom generation.

How did he pull it off, year after year? How did Parks bring together new groups of students and not only discipline them to perform the award-winning, jaw-dropping show that earned them a reputation as the Power and Class of New England, but also motivate them to become better people, thrill them, change them forever?

Sheer voltage, for one thing. "His energy level was just so undeniable, and it was always evident. Always. His commitment was unconditional," recalls Parks's closest colleague and friend of three decades, Thom Hannum, himself nationally celebrated as a percussion arranger and teacher at UMass and elsewhere. Parks marshaled this personal force in a direction that was unrelentingly positive, no matter how challenging the circumstances, says Hannum. "How do you get 350 people to do the same thing? Yeah, you get them to respond to those vocal commands. But his delivery, his teaching style, wasn't somebody barking orders. . . . [It] was always, always positive in nature. It was to find the good that was happening in any situation and highlight that. He was way more than just a performer. The man was a hall-of-fame teacher."

Parks's way of leading left an unforgettable impression on thousands of young people, too. It wasn't about being the boss. It was about serving others to bring out their best. Bogdan, who graduated and went to work as a mechanical engineer in 2011, says in corporate and social life she thinks about this nearly every day. "You watch some people trying

(*continued*)

First the campus was wired for fiber-optic networking, roofs were replaced, and classrooms brought up to date. Building accelerated in the 2000s. Chancellor Lombardi (2002–2007) dubbed this program "New Dirt" and saw it as a way to "reinforce the campus's belief in itself and its future." His tenure saw the opening of a new state-of-the-art Engineering Lab and the groundbreaking for a new Studio Arts Building, a renovated School of Nursing building, and an Integrated Sciences Building. During the tenure of Chancellor Robert C. Holub, who came on in 2008 and served through spring 2012, a beautiful Campus Recreation Center, the George N. Parks Minuteman Marching Band Building, and a major new heating plant lauded for its energy efficiency all opened. A number of upgrades and renovations were completed as well. Groundbreaking for the Commonwealth Honors College complex and new science laboratories and classroom buildings also occurred.

to lead groups and they just don't know how to motivate people," she says. "With George, that 'innocent until proven guilty' idea was taken to an extreme. If we as leaders hadn't taken the time to tell you what we wanted, then it was our fault. Everybody that was in charge of anybody—section leaders, rank leaders, drum majors—was in charge of making the lives of those underneath them better."

Parks, hired to lead the marching band in 1977—along with Hannum, who was brought on in 1984—dramatically revamped the band's artistic style as well, broadening the program from traditional military-style marches based on regular rhythm to incorpo-

...and the band plays on

rate more highly interpreted musical pieces in genres from jazz to pop, often with quicker tempos. Movements blossomed from linear, squad-based formations to a more varied dancelike choreography. The band's performance rose in quality along with complexity, and in 1998 the John Philip Sousa Foundation recognized its excellence by awarding the Minuteman Marching Band its prestigious Sudler Trophy, given annually to one collegiate marching band in the United States.

Parks himself was the driving force behind the campaign to raise support and money for the new state-of-the-art marching band building dedicated in the fall of 2011, just a year after his death. "Enjoy it, take good care of it, and think of George every once in a while as you walk in," Parks's widow, Jeanne, said at the ceremony.

One of the new buildings to result from Chancellor Lombardi's "New Dirt" construction program (left) is the Studio Arts Building.

Holub also oversaw the initiation and completion of a planning process that aimed to engender long-term aesthetic and functional *coherence* in campus development—something that was largely neglected in the fast and furious buildup of the 1960s and 1970s. "You want to preserve the historical character of the campus," says Holub, "while also coordinating green spaces and looking at things like sustainability issues and traffic issues. Without a master plan, you're doing all these things piecemeal."

Dennis Swinford, who in 2010 became UMass Amherst's director of campus planning, says a survey of the university community made it clear that the pond and chapel area remain not only a geographical center but also a spiritual and historical center for the campus. One aim of the campus plan introduced in 2012 is to bring life

The Integrated Sciences Building, also a result of the "New Dirt" program, opened in 2009.

back to the central campus 24/7, with higher density and mixed uses that will draw students for both recreation and study. The pond, for example, "is part of our circulation problem on campus; it's a beautiful landscape but it's also a barrier, a void," says Swinford. "What we've suggested is to create a bridge over the middle of the pond that would allow pedestrians to get back and forth between the two open spaces much more easily. We hope over time that it becomes almost like a little Central Park in the middle of our campus."

PLANTING THE FLAG

For alumni and other friends of the campus to give their hard-earned money to the school reflects pride and a kind of familial commitment to UMass; giving also helps promote these feelings in others. So fundraising has been another area where UMass Amherst has strived to raise its game to a level comparable with the best state schools. Alumni have always

For years predictions have circulated that the digital age would spell an end to "bricks-and-mortar" libraries—dinosaurs like UMass's W. E. B. Du Bois Library, a 28-story redbrick tower built in the early 1970s to house its growing collection of bound-paper volumes. And indeed, as of 2012 the Du Bois Library spends roughly $6 million a year on new materials, the great majority in electronic, not paper, form. Faculty and students can access these materials on their own laptops, nestled in the comfort of their own homes, offices, or dorms.

So why in the world is the library building itself bursting at the seams with under-graduates at all hours of the day and night? Why has the "door count"—the number of people who come into the library each year—doubled since 2005 to about 1.1 million?

The answer lies largely in the library's sprawling, 30,000-square-foot, lower-level complex known fittingly enough as the Learning Commons, which opened in 2005 and has expanded twice since.

(*continued*)

Computers made available to students at the Learning Commons see very little downtime.

The team meeting spaces at the Learning Commons are tailor-made for small-group conferences.

"Commons" is the perfect term for this place where everyone is welcome, and none of the traditional library no-no's are in force. Sip a coffee and nibble a muffin while working at one of the library's hundreds of computers? Certainly. In fact the library café—aptly named the Procrastination Station—sells more coffee than any other place on campus.

Talk on your cell phone? Why not? You're asked to set phones to vibrate, but you can duck into a nearby soundproof booth to take your call.

Work with fellow students around a large table on a common project, chatting and jamming through the night until the thing gets done? Of course. That's what the 25 group rooms are for. And that's why the library is open around the clock from Sunday at 11:00 AM to Friday at 9:00 PM and on Saturday from 9:00 AM until 9:00 PM.

"Fairly soon after we opened the Learning Commons, we had one of our Friends of the Library board members come tour the place," says Jay Schafer, director of libraries at the university. "It was six o'clock on a Saturday night and he was amazed that there were people in the library. He was an alumnus, had been at UMass when Goodell was the library, and he said he always felt like it was the librarian's place. He observed that the Learning Commons really is a student-oriented place. And that's exactly what we wanted it to be."

The Learning Commons is not just an open, welcoming place for students, it's a magnet. They can get all kinds of help from specialized staff there—reference librarians assist in locating materials; writing center peers help whack out a paper or get an essay right; and information technology specialists deal ably with computer glitches of all kinds. "If anything goes wrong with your computer—even your personal computer—you can rush over to them and say, 'My computer has crashed! I've lost my paper! Get it back!'" says graduate student Deliabridget Martinez.

Other schools have computer areas and lounges, but UMass is way ahead in its commitment to the Learning Commons model. "I visited a lot of schools before I came here," says Molly Williams '12, of Medway, Massachusetts. "No other place had what we have here. I had a group project just last week. There were 15 of us in one of those study rooms. We got everything done, and it was just so great to have a meeting place. That's a common thing on campus: 'Meet me at the Learning Commons.'"

On Band Day in 2002, UMass took on Villanova at McGuirk Alumni Stadium.

been avidly involved in certain projects—building playing fields and dorms, for example—but attempts to raise serious money from philanthropists began in 1996 with the five-year Campaign UMass, which sought to raise $125 million. That campaign drew the first seven-figure donation in university history. Since then annual giving has steadily increased. In 2003, friends of the university created the UMass Amherst Foundation with the intention to "match caring people with meaningful opportunities that support both UMass's mission and their personal objectives." Holub's tenure included the campus's first two individual gifts to exceed $10 million and the highest annual giving figure in university history—$57 million.

For some of the top state schools, reputation has everything to do with the classic American sport of football. Games serve as a highly visible show of strength and spirit,

Halftime at Gillette Stadium in Foxborough, the home of Minuteman football for the time being

rallying alumni, getting the school colors and name out to the public, and, ultimately, winning donors, friends with legislative pull, and enthusiastic new students. Starting in the autumn of 2012, UMass Amherst, at nearly 150 years old, stepped into the arena of big-time football, switching from the Colonial Athletic Conference, offering regional competition, to the Mid-American Conference. This conference, which plays in the Division I Football Bowl Subdivision (FBS), represents the top level of college football, its members eligible to compete in high-stakes post-season bowl games against the best teams in the country. UMass Amherst home games have moved temporarily to Gillette Stadium near Boston in Foxborough, Massachusetts, home to the New England Patriots. It holds nearly 70,000 fans; the Amherst campus's Warren McGuirk Alumni Stadium holds only 17,000.

Though the move to FBS football has not been without controversy, UMass leaders believe the change ultimately will be financially prudent and will serve to benefit the campus by diminishing its subsidy. As Holub put it when announcing the change in April 2011, it is "part of our overall move towards ever greater national prominence."

Moving the venue to eastern Massachusetts is part of a larger attempt to establish a greater presence in the state's population center—also the home of many alumni and the seat of state government. In 2010, the Amherst campus opened an outreach office in Boston to cultivate support in the Boston area and in the State House.

A certain tension existed between the power centers of the east and the rural Amherst campus, even during the land-grant college's founding. It has persisted in some form ever since. Chancellors Lombardi and Holub worked hard to maintain the official designation as the *flagship*. Both of these leaders embraced what seems to be a winning formula for securing this status once and for all, which quite simply is *to be* the flagship, claiming the whole state as home ground. A new chancellor, former University of Kentucky provost Kumble Subbaswamy, was selected in the spring of 2012 amid optimism that among his assets is an ability to work well with the UMass system headquartered in Boston.

A class in the Lifelong Learning program, under the auspices of the division of Continuing and Professional Education at UMass Amherst

ACCESS, A SINE QUA NON

UMass Amherst remains at its core a land-grant university with a mission to bring higher education to all people, including those lacking the advantages of wealth and power—people like Manuel Pires, who emigrated from Cape Verde, earned an associate's degree from Roxbury Community College in Boston, then, in 2010, earned a bachelor's in civil engineering at UMass Amherst and went on to graduate work there. The special role of the flagship is to be elite without being elitist, selective without being exclusive.

Transfer from community colleges has long provided a wide road into UMass Amherst, with students who earn an associate's degree with a grade-point average of at least 2.5 guaranteed admission. In 2011 this road got even broader when Chancellor Holub went to Roxbury Community College to announce the UMass Amherst Community College Connection. In this new program, community college graduates with a 3.0 average or higher get full tuition waivers, as well as an array of benefits like special advising and priority for on-campus housing.

Another way into the university for students who can't attend college full time is so-called distance learning. The division of Continuing and Professional Education offers many degree and non-degree programs entirely online. "No need to relocate," says a blurb for the online master's in public health in nutrition program. "Learn at home or anywhere there's a computer with Internet access. Participate at any time of the day or night. Our program fits around your work schedule and other commitments." The division offers other programs at off-campus sites around the state, as well as "blended" programs like the Isenberg master of business administration program where students do some of their coursework online but may also attend classes evenings or weekends in off-campus locations. In 2007, the faculty senate undergirded the quality of online coursework by adopting a policy that, whatever the format, all UMass Amherst classes should meet the same criteria for administration, faculty selection, and overall standards.

Ronnie and Eugene Isenberg

Eugene Isenberg was born in Chelsea, Massachusetts, at the dawn of the Great Depression, to immigrant parents. He was the first in his family to attend college, graduating from UMass Amherst in 1950, during the post–World War II era of growth and opportunity for middle-class Americans.

A person of energy and ambition, Isenberg made more than most of that opportunity, eventually rising to the chairmanship of Nabors Industries, the world's largest oil- and gas-drilling contractor. And he gave back more than most, becoming one of UMass Amherst's most generous donors.

Isenberg and his wife, Ronnie, also a native of Chelsea, have endowed three professorships aimed at promoting interdisciplinary studies in engineering, management, and natural sciences. They have supported a series of scholarships for graduate students working in areas that integrate these disciplines. "This approach," Eugene Isenberg explained in 2005, "is vital to the future economic success of the region and the nation."

The Isenbergs' most substantial gift came in 1997, when they gave a multimillion-dollar gift toward Campaign UMass, a five-year drive to raise $125 million from friends of the university and recruit advocates who would kick up its fundraising to a new level. The Isenberg gift went to a new wing for the School of Management. It indeed set a new standard for giving. Designed as a challenge gift to prompt similar levels of support from the Commonwealth and others, it soon had its effect, with gifts pouring in from other alumni. Isenberg also served a long tenure as president of the UMass Amherst Foundation, founded in 2003 to support private fundraising for the university.

The Isenberg School of Management

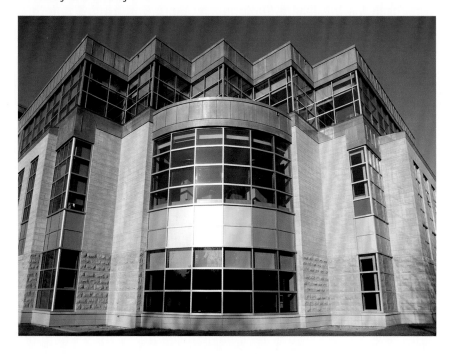

"I believe my own good fortune is, in substantial part, due to the quality and breadth of the education I received," Eugene Isenberg said after making the most substantial of his many gifts to UMass.

UMass leaders, in turn, are convinced that Isenberg's generosity, commitment to public education, and hard work have helped the university rise to the challenges of the twenty-first century. At commencement 2012, Chancellor Robert C. Holub presented Isenberg with the university's inaugural Legacy of Leadership Award to recognize his extraordinary example.

Finally, although more and more the cost of college is a big problem for students—in 2005 the *Boston Globe* called the Amherst campus "increasingly geared toward the affluent"—administrators have tried to offset fee hikes with help for the least well off. UMass Amherst imposed a significant fee increase during the recession year of 2009, for example, but softened the blow by funneling about a third of the increase back into financial aid. During this period the institution has given out a record amount of financial aid and educated the highest number ever of students whose low family incomes qualify them to receive federal Pell grants.

WAYS OF LIFE FOR THE TWENTY-FIRST CENTURY

Whatever the challenges to wide-open access posed by economic and political conditions, UMass Amherst entered its one hundred fiftieth year as a community far more diverse and inclusive than the most fervent republican dreamers of the nineteenth century could have imagined.

As of 2011–12, about 21 percent of both undergraduates and graduate students were members of an increasingly diverse set of ethnic minorities—mainly Asian, Hispanic or Latino, African-American, and multiracial, with a smattering of Native Americans and Pacific Islanders. Of 963 tenure-system faculty reporting race, 213 were non-white, a gain of a few percentage points over 2005–2006.

Diversity of all descriptions remains a constant in each successive twenty-first-century graduating class.

The Amherst campus, though still known for an exercise of free speech that can sometimes get raucous, became less fractious as a community in the opening years of the century, getting officially noticed as "military friendly" by *GI Jobs* while at the same time cited as a "welcoming campus" by an advocacy group for lesbian, gay, bisexual, and transgender people. "I venture to say," Chancellor Holub wrote in a message to the campus community, "that few campuses received praise for inclusivity from such diverse organizations." Whereas in the 1970s students vigorously advocated integration of the sexes in dorms as a way of challenging traditional gender roles, 40 years later students can choose

What if, by some time in the 2030s, temperatures in the area of Pittsburgh, Pennsylvania, became more like the twentieth-century climate of Charleston, West Virginia? Or even that of Knoxville, Tennessee? What would happen to snowpack, spring runoff, water temperatures, rainfall? And what effect would these changes have on wildlife and land use? Which areas would be likely to flood or erode? Presumably, for example, some fish species might no longer find the Connecticut River so hospitable, but others might proliferate there. New invasive plant species might take hold in certain areas. Tourism could suffer in locales that depend on wintertime snow.

The Northeast Climate Science Center (NECSC) based at UMass Amherst is designed to answer just these kinds of questions, modeling climate change and predicting effects, not on a global level, but on a fine-grained local one. That piece largely has been missing from the study of this urgent environmental problem. The data collected by the U.S. Geological Service at tens of thousands of sites, once analyzed by the climate-change center, will be of vital concern to the public agencies and nonprofit groups that manage and steward local land.

"Each of these organizations, in addition to cooperating with us, has some of its own funding from the federal government," explains Richard Palmer, head of the UMass civil and environmental engineering department and university director of the NECSC. "So our job is to focus on the climate aspects of their challenges. These groups are truly resource-management experts, but not climate experts."

The Northeast Climate Science Center is one in a network of eight centers covering different regions of the United States and sponsored by the Department of the Interior. In early 2012, UMass Amherst was given a five-year, $7.5 million grant when it was chosen to lead the consortium of seven universities that comprise the center. The northeast region covers New England and states west to Minnesota and south to Maryland.

Winning the coveted grant to host the climate-change center was a gratifying acknowledgment of Amherst's multidisciplinary research capabilities, and it positions the campus to take a leadership role in future study of climate change.

Left: The fifteenth anniversary of the AIDS Quilt Project was marked in November 2007 at the Student Union Art Gallery. Below: Built in 1949, today Brooks House is among the several specialized residential communities on campus, in this case one for students who want to live in an alcohol-free environment. Bottom: The Ballroom Dance Club's monthly lesson at the Fine Arts Center

from a variety of specialized housing options that put them together with like-minded peers: veterans, first-year students, members of specific ethnicities, people who want to speak a particular language, those who prefer a quiet or drug- and alcohol-free environment, people who are in gender transition—the list goes on.

Sustainability—a concept that implies environmentally friendly lifestyles but also suggests a way of life that sustains community—is something that twenty-first-century students

Members of the UMass Student Farming Enterprise selling their produce at the campus farmer's market

grew up with. They learn the fine points at UMass, an acknowledged leader in this area as one of fewer than a score of universities with a gold star rating from the Association for the Advancement of Sustainability in Higher Education. But it's also something students truly believe in and carry out themselves, taking on projects from the campus permaculture gardens that help supply produce to the dining commons, to the student farmer's market that replaced vending machines in the Campus Center, to the installation of permeable pavers that will help reduce storm runoff outside the visitors center on Massachusetts Avenue. Sustainability is on the agenda of every part of the campus community, from the transit workers to the groundskeepers to the faculty. Dedicated in 2009, the campus's state-of-the-art $133 million Central Heating Plant may not represent the glamorous, high-visibility side of environmentalism, but the award-winning facility packs a punch, reducing UMass's carbon footprint by a whopping 30 percent.

The ubiquity of computers is another reality of the twenty-first-century campus. Computing began at UMass Amherst in the 1960s with big, clunky mainframes designed to serve researchers performing massive calculations. In the 1980s, some students began bringing their own personal computers to school. In the 1990s and 2000s, computing took the campus—and the world—by storm, with students taking up new technologies with enthusiasm, a high-ranked computer science department ready to instruct them, and an Office of Information Technologies on hand to provide equipment and assistance at every turn.

In the 1990s the university replaced its aging telephone system, wiring the campus for Internet connectivity—via a 56 kilobit-per-second connection that a decade later would seem interminably slow. It's hard to believe that as late as the mid-1990s, a student wrote an article in the *Index* titled "Email mania," as if it were a new-fangled invention. "It all begins with the process of getting online," she wrote. "Now, how many of you remember it being fun and easy? I thought so. More like getting your wisdom teeth removed. . . . Sitting at your terminal, you might feel a sense of accomplishment, a sense of pride at finally having made it on-line. Savor it, as it might quickly disappear once you realize that you can't get past the first screen."

Isenberg School of Management students in real time case study classwork

A decade later the campus was fully equipped with wired and wireless high-speed Internet access; an online system for teachers to post syllabi, course material, grades, and sundry other items; as well as an online course catalogue. Librarians were in the process of digitizing many collections, and new materials were largely acquired in digital form. Most campus activities and departments had a web page, and the university was marketing itself through Facebook and Twitter. A hard time getting online? Now it was a challenge for students to get *offline* for a few minutes.

Plagued for years by a reputation as a party school that frustrated the majority of the people who make up the UMass community, the campus has also taken a more serious, public health–oriented approach to problem drinking during the twenty-first century. In 2004 the university created its Center for Alcohol and other Drug Abuse Prevention,

Nearly nine feet long, this handcrafted ceramic-tile mural was created and installed in the University Health Services as a tribute to its staff.

which among other things has required online alcohol education for first-year students and special outreach to athletes. The Campus and Community Coalition to Reduce High-Risk Drinking brings together administration, town, and law enforcement members to address dangerous drinking habits. Among its policy innovations was to ban drinking games and related paraphernalia like funnels and shot glasses. In response to growing awareness about mental health problems among young people, UMass's University Health Services also has stepped up its efforts at suicide prevention and recognition and early treatment of psychiatric emergencies.

In December 2010, UMass professor John M. Gerber blogged about a student who had recently approached him with a rather forlorn question: Why bother? That is, why bother trying to save the world in the face of inevitable declines in nonrenewable oil production, an impending global environmental crisis, and the recent Armageddonlike economic collapse?

Berkshire Permaculture Garden designs (below and opposite, bottom)

Plan View of the Edible Forest Garden
at Berkshire Dining Commons, UMass Amherst
03.22.2012
drawing not to scale

Finally, a major change in the way students approach college in the twenty-first century reflects the increasingly porous boundaries of the university itself—or any place for that matter. Getting some type of field experience—doing at least one internship or "co-op," a temporary unpaid position—has become the norm during undergraduate careers at UMass. Many also study abroad. UMass Amherst was named a "Top Producer of Fulbright Students" (who travel overseas to study under the grant program) by the *Chronicle of Higher Education* in 2009. It ranks third nationally in the number of students securing Gilman Scholarships from the U.S. State Department for study abroad.

The first project, Gerber answered, is to engender hope. Without hope, he said, people just look away from the problem and don't even begin to imagine a solution. So, how could they go about planting that seed of optimism? "Let's grow food," concluded Gerber, who coordinates the Sustainable Food and Farming program at UMass. "Grow food everywhere! Grow food now. Just grow food and teach others to grow food."

As it happens, that very autumn UMass students had literally broken ground on an idea developed in one of Gerber's classes: They had turned an idle quarter-acre of grass by Franklin Dining Commons into a food-producing garden. First they loosened the soil, then spread compost, laid newspaper and cardboard collected from dumpsters to retain moisture, and spread mulch. In all, they raised the ground level 8 to 10 inches, adding some 500,000 pounds of organic matter to the

(*continued*)

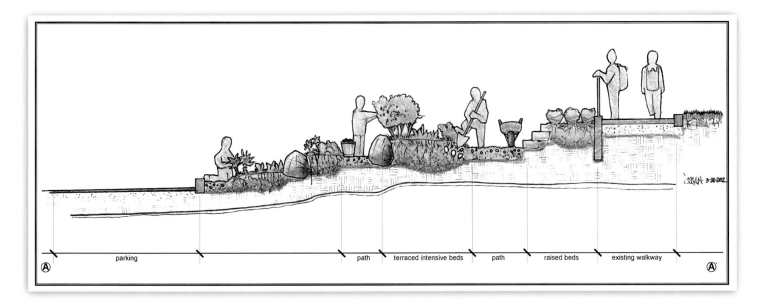

CONTINUITY AND CHANGE

Reassuringly enough, some things never change about the state's public university nestled in the lovely Pioneer Valley. In the autumn, students get down to their studies, faculty to their teaching, under a canopy of flame-colored maples. Winter brings ice-cold nights of cramming for exams. And in the springtime, pressing as the academic calendar may be, with the azaleas and dogwoods abloom, the mood lightens. "Spring's arrival in Amherst was, as usual, a joyous occasion," one 1990s yearbook observed. "Gone were the shivering bodies wrapped in ski jackets and wool coats that made

quarter-acre. "We did it entirely with hand tools, entirely with manual labor, and the only way we were able to do that is because we had so many volunteers," says Nathan Aldrich, who was hired to oversee the project as UMass Amherst's first sustainability coordinator.

That first growing season produced a variety of greens—kale, spinach, mesclun, arugula—as well as tomatoes, peppers, butternut squash, and radishes. The next season would add potatoes, carrots, and beans, as well as an herb garden in a courtyard by Worcester Dining Commons and a new, smaller garden beside Berkshire Dining.

All this fresh-as-it-gets food is served up in the dining commons, though it doesn't come close to supplying the 40,000 meals produced there every day. That's just not in the cards. If the quarter-acre near Franklin Dining were planted entirely in tomatoes, UMass Dining could use them in a day, says Aldrich.

"The food that we produce, while significant in terms of its meaning and origins and impact, is not significant in terms of volume," he says. "We're not feeding this campus and that's not at all the goal. What we can do is educate and get our community involved. We have very visible locations on campus and that's key. It's great if we inspire individuals to get involved in the food system or grow their own food or find out who is growing their food—find a farmer they trust. We're also trying to motivate and serve as a model for other institutions."

everyone look heavy and shapeless. Gone were the eyes that constantly focused on the ground, trying to avoid the invisible patches of ice on pathways of the campus. . . . Suddenly there were smiling faces."

As the land-grant institution approached its sesquicentennial, it seemed to at last shake off the sheepishness of the old Aggies—those farmboys with their calloused hands surrounded by the sons and daughters of privilege receiving a classical education in the area's storied private colleges. UMass is among the upper ranks of like-minded research institutions, state schools proud of their mission of educating citizens to meet whatever challenges

A 12-member student committee is largely responsible for the project, doing everything from coordinating volunteers to managing an active website. Students do the actual gardening, too, with some staying on in summer.

UMass Amherst Auxiliary Enterprises funds the Permaculture Gardens project, having been on board since students first presented the idea in 2009. In fact, thanks in part to the enthusiastic leadership of then–dining services director Ken Toong, in 2011 the dining halls bought more than a quarter of all their produce from local farmers, up from only 8 percent in 2002. That's a feat, given the state's short growing season and the campus's food needs.

As for the campus gardens, they have indeed served as a model: Students, administrators, and dining services people from other schools and colleges regularly come to work in and tour the gardens, and UMass representatives fan out to give talks on how it's done. In March 2012 members of the UMass permaculture garden team visited the Obama White House to receive the Champions of Change award for their work. In June 2012 the campus held a conference called Permaculture Your Campus to spread the word.

Permaculture joins together the words *permanent* and *culture*, pointing to a way of life that's sustainable—that doesn't inexorably deplete natural resources. The founders of Massachusetts Agricultural College, with their "model farm" and scientific methods, would surely have identified with this goal. Though they didn't use words like *permaculture* or *sustainable*, they did concern themselves with the flight of farmers from the state due to the increasing sterility of its soil. They did insist that the people of the Commonwealth could grow food and profit by doing so. They did call agriculture a high calling to which educated young people might return.

Nearly 150 years after Mass Aggie's first students bent their backs to drain campus swamps and pull up roots, UMass students are once again getting their hands dirty—digging the earth that feeds us all.

the age might bring. But the Commonwealth's university in its one hundred fiftieth year also retained the determination, mettle, and resilience of the underdog, which have always been part of its strength.

"The university," as former chancellor Lombardi writes, "is an almost permanent, living enterprise whose existence at any one moment is the cumulative result of its entire history, layered into a campus culture and place over time. A newcomer to a university as significant as UMass Amherst needs to walk the place from one end to the other, through the buildings and along the well-traveled and not-so-often used paths. Such a walk provides a hint of what the place is, has been, and can be."

No single person changes a university with so broad a scope and layered a history. That's the work of many. Lombardi, for one, calls his own twenty-first century tenure at UMass "a lucky moment to see a great place take charge of itself and move."

On July 1, 2012, Kumble R. Subbaswamy became UMass Amherst's new chancellor. Some months later, he mused about the continuity that informs the mission undergirding the university and the diverse changes that this firm foundation has fostered over the past 150 years and continues to support as UMass Amherst forges ahead:

> The vision of our founders and the passion of generations of students and faculty have led to a point where, at the dawn of the twenty-first century, UMass Amherst has come of age.
>
> Ours is a special kind of university, one devoted to the pursuit of academic excellence by the most outstanding students from all walks of life, the quest for research to improve the human condition, and the dedication to serve the Commonwealth and the world beyond. Those qualities, which were central to our founding, are woven into the fabric of our history and give our campus a sense of purpose that defines our faculty, our students, and our alumni.
>
> That sense of purpose is manifested in many ways, not the least of which is the fervor—and boisterousness—with which our campus community expresses ideas and opinions. Vigorous debate has been a hallmark of our history and is vital to the vibrant intellectual environment that we know will thrive at UMass Amherst for generations to come.
>
> One only has to survey the skyline of our magnificent campus, as construction cranes raise new structures skyward, to see that the bold experiment to democratize higher education and serve society that began 150 years ago is alive and well today—and only now has begun to hit its stride.

All told, including the main campus in Amherst and the farm in Hadley plus all the field stations in nine other communities, UMass Amherst covers more than four thousand acres. Close to one-quarter of those comprise the main campus, of which 250 are lawns and another 258 parking lots, all of which are sewn together with 23 miles of roads and 50 of sidewalks. And all of that land, asphalt, and concrete requires careful, regular, nonstop maintenance and attention. Enter the UMass Amherst Buildings and Grounds Services, a crack team of groundskeepers, arborists and landscapers, construction specialists, and many others, who all devote themselves to making sure the large and varied campus remains safe, sustainable, and beautiful.

A recent example exemplifies how adept they are at managing this balancing act: the infamous Halloween nor'easter of 2011. UMass Amherst manager of landscape and construction services Gary Glazier recalls watching carousing, costumed undergraduates wander home from parties amid arcing, crackling downed power lines, describing the scene as "like the Fourth of July." Then there was all that wind and wet, heavy snow weighing down branches still in leaf. The main campus lost countless shrubs and well over 100 trees, from beautiful 200-year-old specimens to newly planted saplings. Months later, groundskeepers were still cleaning up. (On the plus side, downed trees provided 500 cubic yards of woodchips they used to dress campus beds the following spring.)

But that's all part of business as usual for the grounds staff. If a storm's on its way, Pam Monn, physical plant assistant director for building and grounds services, meets with Glazier and other supervisors, and together they lay out a plan for when to bring in the road and sidewalk sanders and decide whether they will need to hire supplemental shovel-wielding workers drawn from other parts of the campus staff to help clear walkways, steps, and building entries.

Come spring, it's time to clean up from winter: fertilize and mend lawns peeled up by snowplows, power-broom the sidewalk edges, prune. As if from hibernation, students emerge from dorms to take part in big events like the Spring *(continued)*

Above: Grounds maintenance crewmembers John Mallow and Jennifer Konieczny work to keep sidewalks clear during a snowstorm. Below: Students plant the 2005 class tree near Goessmann Hall.

Concert or just to sprawl on the grass and soak up the sun. That means even more litter than usual; any given day there are three or four "pickers" at work, making the garbage vanish.

Spring is also a time to fill planting beds with annuals—in 2012 the one on Haigis Mall was all pansies: a field of wine-colored hybrids against which *U* and *M* were picked out in white blossoms. Maybe in summer the staff will rotate in petunias, then mums in the fall. One of the Landscape Management Department's most exciting projects for 2012 was constructing a 40 × 25-foot greenhouse near its Tilson Farm headquarters. According to Glazier, the greenhouse represents the university's first attempt to grow its own annual flowers from seed, potentially saving thousands of dollars a year. Interns from the Stockbridge School of Agriculture, who are gaining invaluable greenhouse experience in the process, undertake this work. "We're learning from them and they're learning as they go along," says Glazier.

The campus is, after all, a teaching arboretum as well as a living and working area. Monn's department provides landscapers and donors with a wishlist of specimens the

campus lacks, with the goal of creating as varied a collection as possible, one that bursts with color throughout the seasons.

In the summertime, when the on-campus population dwindles dramatically, the grounds crew can accomplish big projects as well as tend the lawns and try to make sure they don't dry out too much in hot weather. And as summer turns to dazzling New England autumn, brilliant leaves drifting down with every gust of wind trigger the emergence of massive leaf blowers. The people tending UMass Amherst's campus are hardly immune to the season's beauty, but they're also thinking: Let's get those leaves up before the snows come. "They go to our recycling facility and get put into our compost pile," explains Monn. "Once the compost is cooked, we take it back out and use it in planting new beds and lawns in the spring."

To everything there is a season, and the grounds staff knows well how to take full advantage of this eternal cycle.

UMass Amherst has changed and grown over the past century and half,
from 50 students at its founding to more than 27,000 today.
To be successful and realize our current goals, we must
continue to meet future challenges with a strong physical framework
and a flourishing culture of planning.

— Chancellor Robert C. Holub, 2012

CODA

Campus Plan for the Future

O VER THE PAST SEVERAL DECADES, THE MASTER PLANNING PROCESS HAS BEEN USED IN THOUSANDS OF COMMUNITIES. IT ENGAGES LOCAL CONSTITUENTS, WHO REPRESENT DIVERSE BACKGROUNDS AND VARIED INTERESTS IN THE COMMUNITY, WITH ENVISIONING CHANGE—BOTH BROAD-BASED AND SUBTLE—THAT IS UNDER CONSIDERATION FOR THE TRANSFORMATION OF THEIR BUILT ENVIRONMENT.

UMass Amherst's journey into its third century is both a logical and auspicious occasion for launching a master-planning program, and it officially did so in April 2012. Following best practices for master plan development, the hundreds of participants were well aware that, while nothing they recommended or determined is set in stone, the plan that is emerging accommodates maturation and modulation as it continues to develop.

With its horizon 50 years ahead, the present iteration of the UMass Amherst master plan is certain to change, but as a carefully thought out jumping-off point, it looks openly at how the University of Massachusetts Amherst can grow to support the projected expansion in enrolled students and the increase in faculty and staff expected in the future.

By listening to the university's constituents, the planners are finding ways of assuring that the campus will maintain its bucolic comfort while developing further methods to make its existence increasingly sustainable. Here is a glimpse of a few ways the present plan envisions tomorrow's campus.

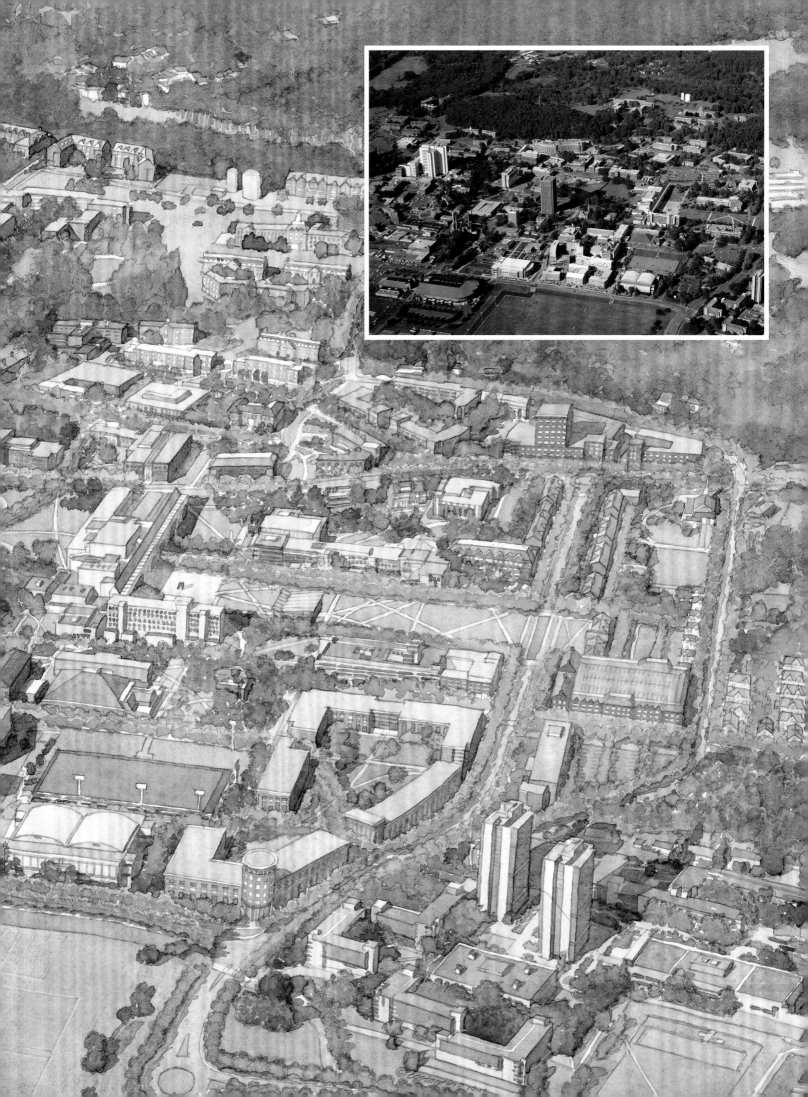

Preceding pages: Center campus as envisioned in the master plan; (inset) aerial photograph showing the same area as it is today

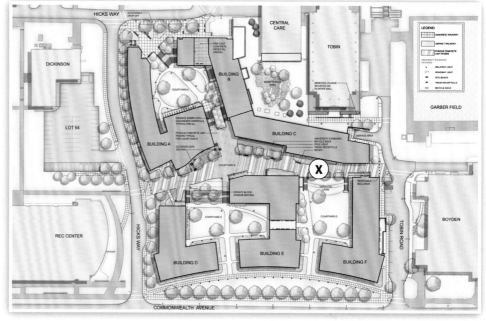

Left and above: Artist's rendering and schematic diagram of Commonwealth Honors College from the master plan

Street-level view of Commonwealth Honors College (*X*s mark approximate location on rendering and diagram)

Massachusetts Avenue as it is ca. 2012 (right) and as envisioned in the master plan (bottom)

Hicks Way 2012 (left) and in the master plan (below)

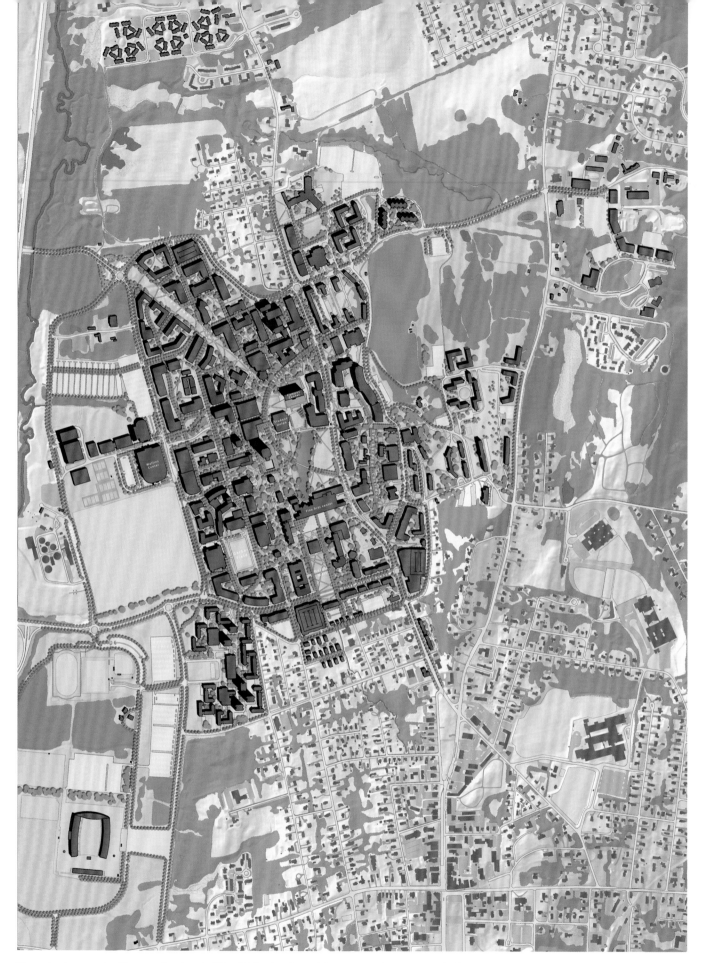

The master plan suggests adding a number of new buildings (brick-red on the map), but preserving the campus's much admired, spacious and open quality by careful siting in relation to the existing structures (brown).

BUILDINGS AT UMASS AMHERST: A REPRESENTATIVE LIST

All buildings on this list are extant as of 2013, and dates in red indicate the year in which each building was completed. Buildings shown in photographs are identified in the listing immediately below them.

1728   **Stockbridge House (University Club)**
Builder: Samuel Boltwood (owner)

ca. 1840   **Montague House**

1869   **Blaisdell House**

1884   **Hillside House (Chancellor's House)**

1885   **South College**
William Brocklesby, Hartford, CT
(renovation 1939 Louis Warren Ross, Architect, Boston)

1886   **Old Chapel**
Stephen C. Earle, Worcester, MA

1887   **West Experiment Station**
Emory A. Ellsworth, Holyoke, MA

1890   **East Experiment Station**
Emory A. Ellsworth, Holyoke, MA

1891   **Hatch Laboratory**

1894   **Horse Barn**

1898   **Munson Hall**
Emory A. Ellsworth, Holyoke, MA

1903   **Draper Hall**
Ellsworth and Kirkpatrick Architects, Holyoke, MA
(addition and conversion 1953 Alderman & MacNeish Architects & Engineers, West Springfield, MA)

1905   **Wilder Hall**
Walter R. B. Willcox, Burlington, VT

1907   **Clark Hall and Greenhouse**
Cooper and Bailey, Boston

•   **Photography Laboratory**
Attributed to James H. Ritchie, Boston

1910   **Fernald Hall and Greenhouse**
Clarence P. Hoyt, Boston

- **French Hall and Greenhouse**
  James H. Ritchie, Boston

1911 **Grinnell Arena**
  James H. Ritchie, Boston
  (abattoir 1929 by Miner J. Markuson Architect, Amherst; band renovation 1997 by Gillen Architects, Amherst)

- **Wysocki House and Barns**

- **Apiary**

1912 **Flint Laboratory**
  James H. Ritchie, Boston

1914 **Stockbridge Hall**
  James H. Ritchie, Boston
  (renovation 1954 McClintock and Craig, Inc., Springfield, MA)

1920 **Nelson House**

1921 **Memorial Hall**
  James H. Ritchie, Boston

1922 **Goessmann Laboratory**
  James H. Ritchie, Boston
  (addition 1959 Appleton & Stearns Architects, Boston)

1923 **Agricultural Experiment Station**
  (renovation 2004 Ford Gillen Architects, Inc., Amherst)

1930 **Chenoweth Laboratory**
  S.S. Eisenberg of Boston (original building and addition 1966)

1931 **Curry S. Hicks Physical Education Building**
  Morse & Dickinson Engineers, Haverhill, MA
  (addition 1987 CBT/Childs, Bertman, Tseckares, and Casedino, Inc., Boston)

1935 **Goodell Hall**
  Morse, Dickinson, and Goodwin, Associated Engineers and Architects, Haverhill, MA (addition 1960 Ames and Graves, Boston)

- **Thatcher House**
  Louis Warren Ross, Architect, Boston

1937 **Bowditch Lodge**
  Volunteers from the 4H community

1939 **Research Administration Building**
  Thomas Byrd Epps Architect, Boston
  (renovation 1988 John Robinson AIA, UMass)

1940 **Lewis House**
  Louis Warren Ross, Architect, Boston

- **Butterfield House**
  Louis Warren Ross, Architect, Boston

1946 **Greenough House**
Louis Warren Ross, Architect, Boston

1947 **Chadbourne House**
Louis Warren Ross, Architect, Boston

1947 **Hasbrouck Hall**
Kilham, Hopkins and Greeley, Architects, Boston
(addition 1963 Desmond and Lord, Boston)

1948 **Middlesex House**
Alderman and Alderman Architects, Holyoke, MA

• **Skinner Hall**
Louis Warren Ross, Architect, Boston
(renovation and addition 2006 Anshen+Allen+Rothman, Boston)

• **New Africa House (originally Mills House)**
Louis Warren Ross, Architect, Boston

• **Berkshire House**
Alderman and Alderman Architects, Holyoke, MA

• **Hampshire House**
Alderman and Alderman Architects, Holyoke, MA

1949 **Brooks House**
Louis Warren Ross, Architect, Boston

• **Gunness Hall**
Appleton & Stearns Architects, Boston

• **Hamlin House**
Louis Warren Ross, Architect, Boston

• **Knowlton House**
Louis Warren Ross, Architect, Boston

• **Lincoln Apartments**
Louis Warren Ross, Architect, Boston

1950 **Paige Laboratory**
Louis Warren Ross, Architect, Boston

• **Marston Hall**
Appleton & Stearns Architects, Boston
(second wing 1954 Appleton & Stearns also)

1952 **Baker Hall**
Louis Warren Ross, Architect, Boston

1953 **Crabtree House**
Louis Warren Ross, Architect, Boston

• **Leach House**
Louis Warren Ross, Architect, Boston

• **Thayer Laboratory**
Louis Warren Ross, Architect, Boston
(addition 1957 Louis Warren Ross also)

• **Worcester Dining Hall**
Morris W. Maloney, Henry J. Tessier Architects, Springfield, MA
(addition 1961 Kilham, Hopkins, Greeley & Brodie Architects, Boston)

1954 **Arnold House**
Louis Warren Ross, Architect, Boston

• **Durfee Conservatory**
Lord and Burnham, Syracuse, NY (original building 1867
T. A. Lord, Syracuse, NY; burned 1883)

1957 **Machmer Hall**
James A. Britton AIA Architect, Greenfield, MA

• **Student Union**
Louis Warren Ross, Architect, Boston

• **Van Meter House**
Louis Warren Ross, Architect, Boston

1958 **Lincoln Apartments**
Louis Warren Ross, Architect, Boston

• **Wheeler House**
Louis Warren Ross, Architect, Boston

1959 **Johnson House**
Louis Warren Ross, Architect, Boston

• **Totman Gym**
Perry, Shaw and Hepburn, Kehoe and Dean Architects, Boston

1960 **Bartlett Hall**
Shepley, Bulfinch, Richardson, and Abbot, Boston

• **Dickinson Hall**
Clinton Foster Goodwin, Architect, Haverhill, MA

1963 **Holdsworth Hall**
M. A. Dwyer Company Architects & Engineers, Boston

1964 **Boyden Physical Education Building**
Morris W. Maloney, Architect, Springfield, MA

1965 **Franklin Dining Commons**
Hugh Stubbins and Associates Inc., Architects, Cambridge, MA

• **McGuirk Alumni Stadium**
Gordon Bunshaft of Skidmore, Owings, and Merrill,
Chicago and New York

1966   **Hampshire Dining Hall**
Hugh Stubbins and Associates Inc., Architects, Cambridge, MA
(renovation 2013 Shawmut Design & Construction, Boston)

•   **Marcus Hall**
Wm. W. Drummey Architects, Boston
(addition 1993 Gunness Engineering Student Center, Kuhn Riddle
Architects, Inc., Amherst)

•   **Morrill Science Center** *(begun 1959)*
Morrill I (1959) and II (1960), James H. Ritchie and Associates,
Architects and Engineers, Boston
Morrill III and Greenhouse (1962), Desmond and Lord Architects, Boston
Morrill IV (1966), Morris W. Maloney, Springfield, MA

1971   **Sylvan Residential Area (Brown, Cashin, and McNamara Houses)**
John Paul Warnecke and Associates, Architects, New York

1967   **Whitmore Administration Building**
Campbell & Aldrich Architects, Boston

1972   **Tobin Hall**
Coletti Bros. Architects, Boston

1968   **Berkshire Dining Hall**
Hugh Stubbins and Associates Inc., Architects, Cambridge, MA
(renovation 2010 Livermore Edwards & Associates Architects &
Planners, Waltham, MA)

1973   **W. E. B. Du Bois Library**
Edward Durrell Stone Architect, New York

•   **Thompson Hall**
James A. Britton AIA Architect, Greenfield, MA

1969   **Herter Hall**
Coletti Bros. Architects, Boston

•   **Lederle Graduate Research Center**
Campbell, Aldrich, and Nulty Architects, Boston

1970   **Murray D. Lincoln Campus Center and Parking Garage**
Marcel Breuer and Associates, Architects, New York

1974   Fine Arts Center
*Kevin Roche, John Dinkeloo and Associates, Architects, Hamden, CT
(lobby addition1999 Perry Dean Rogers and Partners, Architects,
Boston; concert hall elevator and accessible ramp 2001 Kuhn Riddle,
Amherst)*

1988   Robsham Memorial Center for Visitors
KJA Architects, Somerville, MA

1990   Hadley Farm
Carlson & Schmitt Architects, Inc., Agawam, MA

1991   Knowles Engineering Building
Cambridge Seven Associates, Inc., Cambridge, MA

1993   Mullins Center
*Robert Galloway, Cambridge Seven Associates, Inc.,
Cambridge, MA*

1996   Silvio O. Conte National Center for Polymer Research
*Janet Ross, Ellenzweig Associates, Inc., Cambridge, MA;
in association with Whitney Atwood Norcross Associates, Inc.,
Boston*

1999   Computer Science Research Center
Whitney Atwood Norcross Associates, Inc., Boston

**2002   Harold Alfond Management Center addition to
Isenberg School of Management**
ARC/Architectural Resources Cambridge Inc., Cambridge, MA

2004   Engineering Lab II (ELAB II)
*Ellenzweig Associates Inc., Cambridge, MA, in association with
Whitney Atwood Norcross, Associates, Inc., Boston*

2008   **Studio Arts Building**
GUND Partnership, Cambridge, MA

2009   **Integrated Science Building**
*Payette Associates, Inc., Boston; in association with
R. G. Vanderwell Engineers, Inc., Boston;*

  •   **Central Heating Plant**
*Vanderweil, Boston, in association with
Cambridge Seven Associates, Inc., Cambridge, MA*

2011   **George N. Parks Minutemen
Marching Band Building**
Kuhn Riddle Architects, Amherst

  •   **Central Heating Plant**
Vanderweil Engineers and Cambridge Seven Architects

  •   **Campus Recreation Center**
Sasaki Associates, Inc.

  •   **UMass Police Station**
Caolo & Bieniek Associates, Inc., Chicopee, MA

2013   **Commonwealth Honors College**
William Rawn Associates Architects, Inc., Boston

2014   **Academic Classroom Building**
Stantec, Boston

  •   **Life Sciences Laboratory**
Wilson Architects, Inc., Boston

PRESIDENTS AND CHANCELLORS OF THE UNIVERSITY OF MASSACHUSETTS AMHERST

MASSACHUSETTS AGRICULTURAL COLLEGE

1864–66   **Henry Flagg French,**
President

1867 and
1882–83   **Paul Ansel Chadbourne,**
President

1867–79   **William Smith Clark,**
President

1879–80   **Charles L. Flint,**
President

1879 and
1880–82   **Levi Stockbridge,**
President

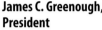

1883–86   **James C. Greenough,**
President

1883 and
1886–1905   **Henry Hill Goodell,**
President

1905–1906   **William Penn Brooks,**
President

1906–24   **Kenyon L. Butterfield,**
President

1924–27   **Edward M. Lewis,**
President

MASSACHUSETTS STATE COLLEGE

1927–32   **Roscoe Wilfrid Thatcher,
President**

UNIVERSITY OF MASSACHUSETTS

1932–46   **Hugh P. Baker,
President**

1947–54   **Ralph Albert Van Meter,
President**

1954–60   **Jean Paul Mather,
President**

1960–70   **John William Lederle,
President**

1970–71   **Oswald Tippo,
Chancellor**

1971–79   **Randolph W. Bromery,
Chancellor**

1979–82   **Henry Koffler,
Chancellor**

1982   **Loren Baritz,
Chancellor**

1982–91   **Joseph R. Duffey,**
Chancellor

1991–93   **Richard D. O'Brien,**
Chancellor

1993–2001   **David K. Scott,**
Chancellor

2001–2001   **Marcellette G. Williams,**
Chancellor

2002–2007   **John V. Lombardi,**
Chancellor

2007–2008   **Thomas W. Cole, Jr.,**
Chancellor

2008–12   **Robert C. Holub,**
Chancellor

2012–   **Kumble R. Subbaswamy,**
Chancellor

INDEX

PICTURE CREDITS

Except for the pictures cited below, all images reproduced in *UMass Rising* are from, and used with permission of: Special Collections and University Archives, University of Massachusetts Amherst Libraries.

Sources for additional images:

Jesús Alvelo-Maurosa: page 113

Archive of *The Daily Collegian*: pages 83 (top), 87 (top), 98 (column 2, middle), 117 (photo by Samantha Webber), 130

Courtesy of Daniel Burke: page 104

Architectural illustrator: F. M. Costantino: pages 142–43 (watercolor)

Jim Gipe/Pivot Media: page 112 (all)

Archive of *The Index*: pages 14, 24–25 (all), 47, 58, 59, 61 (column 1, bottom), 63, 65 (bottom), 77 (bottom), 87 (inset), 96, 97

Library of Congress: page 2 (column 1, top right)

Northeast Climate Science Center (NECSC): page 128

PHENOM (photograph by Ferd Wulkan): page 106

Regenerative Design Group LLC: pages 132–33 (all)

Jeff Stikeman: pages 146 (bottom), 147 (bottom)

U.S. National Archives and Records Administration, Archival Research Catalog: page 2 (column 1, top left)

UMass Amherst Athletics: page 61

UMass Amherst Branding and Creative Communications: pages i–ix (all), x–xi (photo by John Solem), xv; 27, 40, 49 (all), 70, 71, 79 (all), 88 (all), 91 (bottom), 98 (column 1, top and bottom; column 2, top; column 3, all), 99 (column 1, top and bottom; column 2, top; column 3, all), 102 (all), 103 (all), 107 (all), 108 (all), 109 (all), 111 (all), 114, 115, 118–27 (all), 129 (all), 131 (all), 134, 137–39 (all), 143 (inset photo by John Solem), 149–55 (all), 158 (Scott, Cole, Holub, and Subbaswamy)

UMass Amherst Campus Planning: pages 99 (column 2, bottom), 101, 146 (top), 147 (top), 148

UMass Amherst Facilities Planning: pages 144–145

UMass Amherst Student Farming Enterprise (photo by Eric Wheeler): page 130